"When I met Dani
Landing, the place
the leadership of I
there. Daniel spok
confronted Daniel

this information from? This same ʻIo he spoke of, my grandfather shared with me. It was to be kept secret! Who was this guy coming here on our land and talking about ʻIo? I gave him a piece of my mind. As months passed, he gave me a book to read, "Perpetuated In Righteousness." Things came full circle for me. Back to the place of understanding of the One True God, ʻIo. I had experienced the Aloha ʻIo had for our people. Then I realized that Daniel had the same heart and compassion for the Hawaiian people, as ʻIo, our One True God. I experienced the Aloha of ʻIo flowing within Daniel's heart. His expression of God's Aloha flowed within me. I challenge you to read this book. It led me to search out the Bible to see if Daniel's words were pono, in plumb line with the Bible. Yes it is! Aloha Ke Akua!"

**Mickey Ioane**
*Writer and Composer of the Song "Hawaiʻi '78"*
*Given to His Friend, Israel Kamakawiwoʻole*
*Voted One of the Top 50 Songs in Hawaiian Music History*

---

"Daniel Kikawa is a spiritual Wayfinder re-tracing the ancient knowledge and paths of our ancestors. This book inspires me to teach the next generation to be proud of and thankful for the culture our God gave to us in His great Aloha for us. This same God of Aloha is the God of the Bible my kupuna recognized, accepted, loved and followed."

**Kalani Kahalioumi**
*Hōkūleʻa Navigator/Captain*
*Voyaging Canoe Builder*

---

"Kalo (Taro) will only grow healthy if the water is fresh, clean and flowing. The water from the loʻi (Taro patch) above must flow to the one below and so on for it to be healthy. So must the "Water of Life" flow from Heaven to our Kūpuna and to the next generation for future generations of our people to be healthy. I composed the music for He Waiwai Nui written by my cousin Lehua Kawaikapuokalani Hewitt about this important concept. The chorus of the song says, "Ola ka Hā (Life from the Spirit of God), Ola ka Wai (Life from the Water of Life, Iesū), Ola ka ʻĪ (Life from the Supreme God, ʻIo)." This is, HaWaiʻĪ, the name of the ʻaina that ʻIo gave our people to

kahu (be caretakers of). May our people return to their true God of
Aloha so the Living Water will again flow freely."

**Kahu Kawika Kahiapo**
*Multiple Nā Hōkū Hanohano Music Award Winner*
*Lifetime Achievement Award for Slack Key Guitar*

---

"There is no greater authority that I know in regards to the genealogy
and anthropology of the Polynesian people when it comes to a Christ-
centered perspective than Dr. Daniel Kikawa. Dr. Kikawa captured
my imagination with Perpetuated in Righteousness in my mid-20's
and gave a theological, archaeological framework to the origins of
the concept of a One True God before the Kapu System and up until
the first missionaries arrived in these islands over 200 years ago.
You will be enlightened and awakened to the history of faith of the
Hawaiian people and be in wonder and awe of God's love for all
humanity."

**Kahu Mike Kai**
*Founder and Senior Pastor, Inspire Church Network*
*Founder, Influencers' Network*
*Author, International Speaker*

---

"Nainoa Thompson and Hōkūleʻa re-established our Hawaiian
and Polynesian identity as great ocean navigators. Our story as
Wayfinders was lost for a time. We forgot we had relationship with
the heavens, the stars, the winds, the swells, the birds and more.
Nainoa helped us to remember. Wayfinder Kahu Daniel Kikawa
helps us remember... something much more profound. We forgot
our ancestors had relationship to the very Source and Creator of all
things, and we knew him by name. This story too was lost for a time
and Kikawa re-connects the ancient paths. A renaissance of aloha is
promised as we re-establish our identity in ʻIo."

**Kahu Kihapiʻilani (Kiha) Pimental**
*Associate District Superintendent*
*Pacific Southwest District, International Foursquare Church*
*Supervisor, Global Missionary Support, International Foursquare*
*Church*

---

"A fabulous read! Maikaʻi! This book will reveal ʻIo to you in many
different lands and different ways."

**Kaipoʻi Kelling**
*Hawaiian Language Kumu, Author, Songwriter, Chanter*

"Kahu Daniel Kikawa has done the good work, ka hana maikaʻi in his latest literary exploration of ʻĪo. Kahu utilizes the whole gamut of scholarly tools to examine the cultural brilliance of our lāhui and their ancient knowledge and worship of the one and only omnipresent God. Pōmaikaʻi ka lāhui kanaka, ʻo Iēhova kona Akua; ka poʻe kanaka hoʻi āna k koko ai i hoʻoilina nona.
We are a chosen people, and we are a nation of a blessed inheritance."

**Kahu Brian Kaunaloa Boshard**
*Ordained Minister, HIAUCC and UCC*
*Ka Moku o Keawe*

---

"In The True God of Hawaiʻi – The Case for ʻĪo. Daniel Kikawa continues to expand on his collection of accounts of the Polynesian's One True God, bringing to light, in particular, many sources across the Hawaiian Islands."

**Christopher "Chris" Cook**
*Author of The Providential Life & Heritage of Henry Obookiah*

---

"This is a  must read, Daniel Kikawa's personal knowledge and research of ʻĪo gives us a deep insight into the Hawaiian culture."

**Rev. (Kahu) David de Carvalho**
*Mokuaikaua Church*
*The historic first church of Hawaiʻi*

---

"When Noah and his family stepped out of the Ark, 'And God blessed Noah and his sons and said to them, "Be fruitful and multiply and fill the earth" (Genesis 9:1); at that point in time, the ancestors of all human generations knew of the one and only Creator of all things. Therefore, is it too much of a stretch to think that cultures around the world including Hawaiʻi and Polynesia would have recessed within it, the knowledge of the one and only Creator described in the Bible, albeit through a Judeo-Christian lens?  And like the Israelite remnant described in the Bible, who held steadfast to the knowldge of the One Creator God through oppressive and waning times, is it too much of a stretch to believe that there would remain a knowing and believing remnant of the One Creator God in other cultures? What Kahu Daniel Kikawa has put forth in his book series of ʻĪo, and ʻĪo's relation to Hawaiʻi, has revealed how the pattern of Israel's knowing and waning of God played out here in Hawaiʻi nei. It is a place-based example of God's ongoing story here in these islands (Acts 17: 26-27).

The challenge now for the church here in Hawai'i is twofold, will we believe that we have a place specific connection to the Creator, and if so, how will that place specific knowledge of God glorify the Creator and impact the world for good through Aloha?"

**Kamuela Plunkett**
*B.A. - Anthropology, Archaeology*
*M.A. - Heritage Management*

---

"Amazing! 'The True God of Hawai'i' is Daniel Kikawa's best work. We are in a time of real revival, especially among indigenous people; and they are hungry for real answers. They will find them in this book!"

**Kahu Greg Dela Cruz**
*Living Way Church Maui*
*Instructor: Kamalama*
*Ho'oponopono Practitioner*

---

"Daniel Kikawa has found a way to help us overcome the difficulties, differences and divide in Hawai'i; while moving forward into the future. That way can be found in the most important treasure, word and purpose for the people of Hawai'i and Polynesia captured in this amazing book."

**Kahu Allen Cardines**
*Sr. Pastor, Nānāikapono Church*
*Transform Our World Hawai'i*

---

"Kahu Daniel Kikawa has always been an inspiration to the many of us that have been searching for more insight on Hawaiian HIS-story! This book will confirm, inspire and unveil revelation knowledge of the One True God that the early Hawaiians worshiped. They did it with the divine Aloha given to them from above."

**Kahu Matt Higa**
*Descendant of Hewahewa*
*New Hope Kauai Senior Pastor*
*Kauai Foursquare District Superintendent*
*Hawai'i Pastors' Round Table*

---

"Many people are writing books today. This is a good thing. There are many insights that need to be shared and stories to be told. And there are those authors whom God raises up who not only have great stories and great insights but their insights and stories transform the world and our culture for the better. Daniel Kikawa is one of them. His books have changed the way we view God and what He is like. His insights and stories have changed our culture for the better. Daniel has shown us that God is not some far-away foreign God but, as the Apostle Paul declared to the polytheistic Athenians, the one true God 'is not far from any of us' (Acts 17:27). Daniel reminds us again and again that God is not some Western 'foreign' God but is the Creator of us all and has revealed Himself to every people group as their God, as THE GOD."

**Kahu Cal Chinen**
*Pacific Region Superintendent*
*Missionary Church USA*
*Transform Our World Hawai'i*

---

"In this book, Daniel shares what many Hawaiians (Kanaka Maoli) know in their heart is true. History, both Hawaiian and Biblical, confirms the Aloha, Ke Akua has for us. Take your time while reading and allow our Creator God to create in you a clean heart filled with Aloha."

**Kahu John L. Trusdell, Jr.**
*Descendant of Hewahewa*
*Ordained, Hawaii Assemblies of God*
*Presbyter, Big Island Section*

---

Daniel Kikawa is at once a pastor, a historian and a researcher. He is the Senior Pastor at the HMC 'Ohana Church and the Kaimu Hale Pule. He is also a meticulous historian and researcher who passionately pursues his specialty which is discovering, interpreting and teaching on his findings which he has confirmed again and again; that God has proactively put "eternity into the hearts" (Eccl. 3:11) of the peoples of the Pacific.

In 1955 the "Father of the Church Growth Movement," Donald McGavran, wrote an epic book entitled The Bridges of God. In it he pointed out that God has sovereignly placed in various cultures certain clues that point to the One True God and demonstrate his desire to reach every people and nation. A generation after McGavran another researcher, Don Richardson, who had spent 15 years among the Sawi tribe in Irian Jaya, demonstrated and confirmed McGavran's thesis in his book Peace Child. Confirming the proactive bridges that God has built for people to cross in pursuit of truth. Richardson became one of Daniel's mentors as well as mine. Richardson's book Eternity In Their Hearts chronicles twenty-seven case studies of these cultural clues that are within the cultures of many peoples of the earth. God's general revelation to prepare people for his special revelation in the Bible is clear. Daniel has now added to McGavran and Richardson's work as well as to his own previous contributions, Perpetuated In Righteousness and God of Light, God of Darkness. Daniel has done us all a favor by teaching us how to navigate ancient traditions which could be interpreted as "pagan" to the casual reader when in reality, to the inquiring and hungry person, may indeed be a Bridge of God.

Any person who seeks to discover Paul's admonition to us to "… be all things to all men that by all means we might reach some" (1 Corinthians 9:22) will run into those forks in the road pointing us to either syncretism (compromise of the message of Jesus) on the one hand and a proper contextualization that fits not only the biblical narrative but discovers what God has been doing in a culture before the missionary gets there. Someone has said that the missionary does not take God to native people. God is already there before the missionary shows up, Eternity In Their Hearts! Daniel has used his God-given skills to circumvent the syncretism trap but is not shy about boldly proclaiming his findings through extensive research drawn from original sources.

Those of us who live in the Pacific, particularly Hawai'i, will be indebted to Daniel for his painstaking research. His careful interpreting of the facts will, by God's grace, lead many people in the islands to pursue the One True God. So my advice is, get yourself a cup of Kona coffee, sit back and be blessed. Daniel has done the heavy lifting. All we have to do is feast on what he has prepared for us. You are in for an adventure!

**Danny Lehmann**
*Dean, College of Christian Ministries*
*University of the Nations/YWAM*

# The True God of HAWAI'I

# The Case for 'Io

Daniel Kikawa, Ph.D.
(Intercultural Studies)

*The True God of Hawai'i*
*The Case for 'Io*
Copyright 2021 © by Daniel Kikawa
All Rights Reserved

To request permissions, contact the publisher at www.alohakeakua.org

Published by:
Aloha Ke Akua Publishing
www.alohakeakua.org

Text and cover design by Pine Hill Graphics

Cover Photo: Lo'iloa, 'Iao Valley, Maui by Kahu Daniel Kikawa
Kalo (Taro) will only grow healthy if the water is fresh, clean and flowing. The water from the lo'i (Taro patch) above must flow to the one below and so on for it to be healthy. So must the "Water of Life" flow from Heaven to our Kūpuna and to the next generation. From the song, He Waiwai Nui by Kawaikapuokalani Hewitt and Kawika Kahiapo. "Ola ka Hā (Life from the Spirit of God), Ola ka Wai (Life from the Water of Life, Iesū), Ola ka 'Ī (Life from the Supreme One, 'Io)" HaWai'Ī.

ISBN 978-0-9643595-2-9

Printed in the United States of America

# Dedicated to:

The Hawaiian People whose Aloha the world needs now. For my hānai brother, Cleigh "Ākea" Eaton and mom Arlene Eaton. Ka Baibala says, "We love (Aloha) Him (God) because He first loved (Aloha) us." 1 John 4:19 KJV. So did you and mom Aloha me first.

Ākea Eaton

**In Memory of:** Cleighton Kalaninuiakea Eaton, Mom Arlene Wainaha Eaton, Auntie Malia Kawaiho Ouluoha'ao Craver, Uncle Bill Kalikolehua Panui, Auntie Dolly Moke, Kahu Gaymond Apaka, Kahu Henry Kahalehili, Don Richardson, Kahu Ken Kekoa, Kahu John Kalili, Don Mapes, Kahu Paul Kamanu, Don Kealoha Ahia, Melani Werohia, Robert Kikawa

**Maori:** Charlie Mathews, Monte Ohia, Meto Hopa, Tomas Watene Rosser, Huikakahu Kawe

**Mahalo Nui:** Yolanda Kikawa, Kumu Hula Moses Kaho'okele Crabbe, Carmelita Kinau "Dutchie" Kapu Saffery, Leon Kāulahao Siu, Kahu Kawika Kahiapo, Kumu Hula Namahana Panui, Kumu Kaipo'i Kelling, Kahu Kaeo DeCoite, Danny Lehmann, Kahu John Trusdell, Curtis Malia, Kaleo Haleakalā, Kahu Kihapi'ilani Pimental, Jill Paresa, Chris Cook, Kahu

Leifi Leiolani Haʻo, Kamuela Plunket, Kahu Hanalei Colleado, Margaret Harryman, David Heaukulani, Kahu Matt Higa, Kahu Wendell B.K. Davis, Kahu Mike Kai, Kahu Cal Chinen, Kahu Allen Cardines, Kahu Greg Dela Cruz, Kahu David De Carvalho, Kalani Kahalioumi, Mickey and Pattie Ioane, Kumu Hula Leihiʻilani Kirkpatrick, Kaleo Waipa, Hanale and Zhan Dudoit, Kahu Jonathan Steeper, Peter Young, George Kāimiola, Miles Matsumura, Nalu and Kanani Kay and ʻOhana, the Sons of Yeshua, Island Breeze, Leinaʻala Fruen, Kawewehe Pundyke, Keala Pule, Kahu Moanikeʻala Nanod-Sitch, Kahu Jonah Kaʻawai, Kahu Jason Kerr, Sam Keliʻihoʻomalu, Kahu Cameron Hiro, David Garratt, John Dawson, Matt Dawson, Gary and Kaʻila Williams, Gail McConnell,

**Maori:** Huikakahu Kawe, Eruera Kawe and Kawe Whanau, Bishop Whanau and Kaumatua of Kawhia, Peneamine Whirohia, Ray Totorewa, Brad Haami, David and Denise Moko, Tehurihanga Rihari, Graham and Tui Cruikshank, Wihongi Whanau, Paul Norman, Michael Faʻamoana Toʻo, Dr. Cathy Moana Dewes, Brent Eru

Special thanks to the Kingitanga (Maori King's Office) for permission to include information from Turongo House about the Maori Kings.

**Samoan:** Special thanks for writing the Samoan portion of this book to: Aliʻi Tagaloa Lupematasila Vaeluagaomatangi Elisara Sao Filioalii in consultation with Chief Misa Teleiʻai of Falelatai/Sāmatau ʻUpolu Sāmoa and Chief Matuāvao Tualāina Meafua of Sāleʻaula Sāvaii Sāmoa.

This book is a collaboration of the knowledge, gifts, skills, and research of many people. Me ka naʻau haʻahaʻa, mahalo nui me ke aloha palenaʻole, Daniel Kikawa

# Table of Contents

# Glossary

Akua – A god, a spiritual being
Ali‘i – Chief/Chiefess, Royal
Hā – Spirit, breath, life
Ha‘a – Ancient form of hula
Heiau – temple
Hānai – Adopted child, can be temporary or permanent
Kahu – Pastor, caretaker
Kahuna – Priest, expert in a skill
Kāhuna – Priests (plural)
Kahuna Nui – High priest
Kaona – Underlying hidden/secret meaning within
    Hawaiian chants and songs
Kapu – Taboo, can mean restricted, forbidden or sacred/holy
Kāula – Prophet
Kupuna – Respected elder
Kūpuna – Respected elders (plural)
Lōkahi – Unity, harmony
Maka‘āinana – Common people
Makutu – Maori Witchcraft
Mana – Spiritual power
Maori – Native people of Aotearoa (New Zealand)
Noa – Free from restrictions
‘Ohana – Family
Pele – The volcano goddess
Pono – Righteous, in perfect order

Pono Ones – The most righteous child in each generation to
whom the secret knowledge of 'Io was passed
Tohunga – Maori kahuna, priest, expert in a skill
Wai – Fresh Water

## Names of Historical People, Gods, Places and Things of Significance

Aotearoa – Maori name for New Zealand

Baibala Hemolele – Hawaiian Holy Bible

Buck, Peter (Te Rangi Hiroa) – Polynesian anthropologist, historian and scholar (1877-1951)

Fornander, Abraham – Polynesian ethnologist, historian and scholar (1812-1887)

Handy, Craighill – Polynesian ethnologist, historian and scholar (1892-1973

Hewahewa – Last High Priest of the Kapu System (1774-1837)

Iesū - Jesus

'Io, 'Ia, I'o, 'Ī, Io, Kiho, Kio, Eho, Iho, Ihoiho, Ioa – Polynesian dialects of the name of the first, true, Creator God of Polynesia

Ka'ahumanu – Kamehameha's favorite wife (1768-1832)

Ka Lae – Southernmost point of the Big Island, Hawai'i

Kalākaua – Hawaiian Historian, Scholar and Last King of Hawai'i (1836-1891)

Kalanimoku – Prime Minister (1768-1827)

Kamakau – Hawaiian Historian and Scholar (1815-1876)

Kamehameha – Chief who unified the Hawaiian islands (1738-1819)

Kapihe – Famous Kāula

Kapu System – Religious System brought to Hawai'i by Pā'ao

Kauikeaouli – Kamehameha III (1814-1854)

# Glossary

Keauhou – A place on the Big Island of Hawai'i, meaning:
   The New Era
Ke'ōpūolani – Kamehameha's sacred wife (1778-1823)
Kepelino – Hawaiian Historian and Scholar (1830-1878)
Kū – A major god
Liholiho – Second King of Hawai'i (1797-1824)
Lili'uokalani – Hawaiian Historian, Scholar and Last Queen
   of Hawai'i (1838-1917)
Malo – Hawaiian Historian and Scholar (1795-1853)
'Ōpūkaha'ia – First Hawaiian Christian (1792-1818)
Pā'ao – Legendary Tahitian Priest who changed the religious system of Hawai'i
Pākī, Pilahi – Respected Hawaiian Cultural practitioner
   (1910-1985)
Potatau Te Wherowhero – First Maori King (1770-1860)
Pukui, Mary Kawena - Respected Hawaiian Cultural practitioner, Historian and
Scholar (1895-1986)
Tawhiao, Tukaroto Matutaera – Second Maori King
   (1822-1894
Taylor, Ahu'ena – Hawaiian Historian and Scholar
   (1867-1937)
Whare Wananga – Maori House of Sacred Learning

Some Hawaiian words like "Aloha" and "Kupuna" are capitalized at times to emphasize the importance and respect they have in the Hawaiian.

Quotes from the 1800s and early 1900s had no "'okina" or "kahakō" markings, I have left them as they were written. When quoting sources from this era, I have also not changed the old English spelling of words or modernized words that are no longer used.

# Preface

A loha Kākou Ē! Welina mai me ke Aloha!

Dear Reader,

This book is the culmination of over 35 years of research and interviews. It is written for the people of Hawai'i. Therefore, it is written more in the style of a kupuna talking story to 'ohana than as a dissertation for college professors. It is meant to be more personal than academic and impersonal. However, like an academic paper, the information within has been thoroughly documented and footnoted.

I am a Kahu, so I view history through the premise that there is a Creator. Just as secular humanists view history through the premise that there is no Creator, just an evolutionary process. All writers are subjective in one way or another. There is no truly objective writer. All evidence is interpreted through his or her lens. Therefore, the information in this book is interpreted through my premise that there is a Creator God.

I will be using both written and oral sources for my information. Many *Kuana'ike Haole* (European/American trained thinkers) are taught to value only what has been written. This type of thinker believes oral sources are "*hearsay*" and unreliable even though oral sources are considered primary sources by historical researchers. Oral primary sources (as well as all primary sources) are subjective according to the person who is interpreting the information. However, the more sources that repeat the same or similar information, the more reliable that information is. The reader will find that with all the primary and secondary sources attesting to the ancient knowledge of One Creator God in Polynesia, the evidence is substantial.

Many do not understand that the ancient Polynesians (as well as other oral cultures) had special experts (kāhuna) who were selected for their memory and then endured rigorous training. They were trained to recite long chants that, if written, would take hundreds of pages. These chants needed to be chanted exactly. It is not like playing the *"telephone game"* where distortion comes very quickly to untrained minds. Tomas Watene Rosser (deceased) met a Maori Tohunga (Kahuna/priest, expert in a skill) who had a large volume that contained long chants. The Tohunga told Tom to open the book anywhere and begin reciting the portion of the chant he saw there. Each time Tom began a portion of the chant no matter where it was in the large volume, the Tohunga finished that portion of the chant exactly.

Another reason I use many oral sources is that many *Kuana'ike Hawai'i* (Hawaiian/Native Thinkers) value primarily what is orally passed down by the kūpuna. This is because Hawaiians were an oral society with no conventional written language. All important information was passed down to the 'ohana from kūpuna (elders to the next generation) or from kumu to haumana (teacher to student). Even when writing came, the most sacred information was passed down from elders to selected students or descendants. The most sacred family knowledge was not written where anyone, especially those who may not respect the Hawaiian people, might read and ridicule. When *Perpetuated In Righteousness* was first written, Leon Kāulahao Siu took the book to a Hawaiian cultural practitioner. The cultural practitioner asked what our sources were. Leon told him, *"Written and oral sources."* This man replied, *"I will read it because you use oral sources."* Many Hawaiians mistrust written sources because much of what was written about Hawaiian history was not true and/or was propaganda, this will be explained in this book. Hawaiian skepticism of written sources is, therefore, understandable.

In this book, I will not be including the names of some primary oral sources or specific details about their information. Those sources either did not give me permission to use their names or they desired that their family names remain anonymous. Some will not understand this because, to them, I have just voided my credibility by not listing my sources. However, many Hawaiians will give my information even more credibility because my sources deemed me trustworthy not to divulge their secrets. Many may not understand why a person would not like to be noted in a book. I chastised an author to whom I gave information because she put the names of these sources in her book without first obtaining permission from them. She said she thought they would be thrilled to have their names in a book. She said anyone on the Mainland would. However, many Hawaiians and other native people are not excited to be in a book, on the contrary, it can take mana (spiritual authority) from them. They believe that their most precious information should not be out in public but be for the chosen ones who will be pono (righteous with the information). This is why I am very careful about what is recorded in this book and have not included many of the most intimate/precious details. If information or statements are on public record; YouTube, a public website or in a published book, etc. I have cited this information that has been made available to the general public.

I also use many Maori sources. As I will explain more thoroughly in the course of this book, many Maori claim they came from Hawai'i. Not only the Polynesian tradition of coming from *Hawai'i Nui, Hawai'i Loa, Hawai'i Pāmamao* (There are different traditions about where these are) but that they left specifically from Ka Lae, South Point of the Big Island. Their genealogies, chants and traditions also confirm that they came from Hawai'i.

Many of the items I will explain within, I realize are very elementary to many readers. E kala mai, just skip over these areas, it is not meant for you. It is meant for those who have little background in Hawaiian history and culture. Sadly, I have found many in Hawai'i, Hawaiians and non-Hawaiians, know very little about Hawaiian history and culture.

Aloha Pumehana,
*Daniel Kikawa*

# Chapter 1

# The Importance of ʻĪo to the Hawaiian People

In Hawaiʻi, most of our educational institutions only teach about the *Kapu System* as the religion and culture of Hawaiians. Very little, if anything, about the God, ʻĪo, is taught.

If there was no God, culture or religion before the gods, culture and religion of the *Kapu System*; then where did the concept of Aloha come from?

## The Kapu System

There was little Aloha in the religion of the Kapu (as in "*Forbidden*") System which was brought to Hawaiʻi by a latter migration. More about the Kapu System in later chapters. For instance, men and women were forbidden to eat together. If they did, they were all killed, no grace or mercy was given. Women were forbidden to eat bananas, coconuts and pork among other things. Even if a little girl,

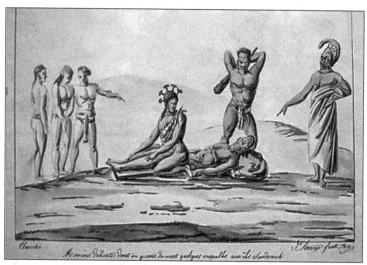

Death of a Kapu Breaker

who did not know any better ate one, she was killed without grace or mercy. If even a shadow of a commoner fell on an aliʻi (chief) by accident, the commoner was killed. If a commoner stepped on aliʻi lands by accident because the lands were not marked, he was killed without grace or mercy. There was no forgiveness of these "sins."

Is this who Hawaiians are? Or are Hawaiians the people of Aloha? What is Aloha?

## Aloha

Aloha is:

"*Akahai*" – Tender Kindness

"*Lōkahi*" – Unity in harmony and peace

"ʻ*Oluʻolu*" – Graciousness (as in unmerited favor and mercy)

"*Haʻahaʻa*" – Humility

"*Ahonui*" – Patience and Long suffering

This description of Aloha was given by *Pilahi Pākī*, a close friend of Leon Kāulahao Siu, a co-founder of Aloha Ke Akua. Pilahi Pākī was one of the most respected and beloved kupuna (deceased), known for her Aloha and her knowledge of Hawaiian culture. All of these words describing *"Aloha"* are aspect of *Agape* or Godly Love. Aloha is the embodiment of Perfect Love. These descriptions of Aloha cannot be accomplished without empathy, grace (unmerited favor and mercy) and compassion; which are all aspects of Aloha. Aloha is so deeply spiritual that all of these words still do not do it justice.

All of these descriptions of Aloha also cannot be

achieved without forgiveness. Queen Liliʻuokalani's favorite scripture was, "(God) *Forgive us our trespasses, as we forgive those who trespass against us.*" (Mat. 6:12). She would compare this scripture with an old Hawaiian proverb, *"No one is free from their own sin, until they have forgiven those who have sinned against them."*

My kūpuna taught me that when they were young, when the sacredness of "*Aloha*" was still understood, one could not even speak the word, "*Aloha*," if there was any hate, bitterness, anger or unforgiveness in his heart. He would have to cleanse himself before even speaking the sacred word, "*Aloha*."

Today, the sacredness of the word, "*Aloha*," has been lost. It is now yelled out at some lū'au shows without the meaning of the word being taught. It is also sometimes placed in names of businesses without understanding the responsibility that comes with calling one's business "*Aloha* _____*". Aloha is now spoken at times with bitterness and unforgiveness in the heart and without love for all people. I was taught that you either Aloha or you don't Aloha. You must Aloha everyone, you cannot Aloha some and not others. You can hate what some people do but you must Aloha them. The depth and sacredness of Aloha is no longer taught to many who live in Hawai'i today. Because of this secularizing of the word, "*Aloha*," a term I had never heard from my kūpuna is being used today, "*Kapu Aloha*." "*Kapu*" as in "*Sacred or Holy*," not as "*Forbidden*." I agree with the term; it has become necessary to distinguish true Aloha from the secular degraded one.

My kūpuna and mentors taught me "*Aloha Ke Akua*," "*God is Aloha*," and compared it to the scripture, "*E nā punahele, e aloha kākou i kekahi i kekahi: no ka mea, no ke Akua mai ke aloha; 'o ka mea e aloha aku ana ua ho'ohānau 'ia mai ia e ke Akua, a ua 'ike nō 'o ia i ke Akua. 'O ka mea e aloha 'ole ana, 'a'ole ia i 'ike aku i ke Akua; no ka mea, he Aloha ke Akua*." Ka Baibala Hemolele. "*Beloved, let us love one another, for love is of God; and everyone who loves* *is born of God and knows God. He who does not love does not know God, for **God is Love**."* 1 John 4:7-8 NKJ.

Aloha is the *"Spirit of the Living God"* with us. *"Alo"* – In the Presence of, *"Hā"* – *"The Holy Breath of Life."* Who is this God of Life?

# Chapter 2

# Who is ʻĪo?

ʻ*Ī o*," in some Hawaiian dialects called "*ʻĪa*," *Iʻo* or simply "*ʻĪ*," is the name of the Creator God of Hawaiians and Polynesians. *ʻĪo* is also known as *Io, Kiho, Kio* (The Hawaiian "*okina*" is "*K*" in some Southern Polynesian dialects), *Eho, Iho, Ihoiho,* and *Ioa* in other Polynesian dialects. He is the original/true Creator God of Polynesia. Evidence for this will unfold in future chapters.

No kiʻi (tikis, idols) were ever made of ʻĪo. He had many titles that described his nature. One was *ʻĪo-Matua-Kore* (Maori - *ʻĪo Makua ʻOle* in Hawaiian) meaning, *ʻĪo the One without Parents,* connoting *The Uncreated One.* All the other "*gods*" of Polynesia were created or were descendants of others. He was also called, *ʻĪ-lala-ʻole* (*ʻĪo Without Branches*), meaning he had no wife and (no sexually procreated) children. The other "*gods*" of Polynesia had wives and procreated descendants.

Maori traditions say that ʻĪo had no origin and will know no end. "*He was, and is, Io the Eternal.*" He always existed.

27

He had no parents, wife or children. He was *'Io-Mataaho,* *"Man can view Io only as he sees radiation of light, he cannot actually see him."* *"We have seen that no form of image or representation of Io was ever made by the Maori, such an act was inadmissible."* No sacrifices or offerings were made to 'Io nor did he have any visible form or form of incarnation (kino lau). 'Io had nothing to do with anything evil.[1]

Man was sacred to 'Io and not to be killed. During the time when Hawaiians worshipped 'Io, Hawaiian society was peaceful and the ali'i were like parents to the maka'āinana, the common people. According to various kūpuna, 'Io was worshipped from about 400AD to 1100 - 1300 AD when the powerful *kahuna* (priest) *Pā'ao* came to Hawai'i and introduced the *Kapu System.* More on Pā'ao and the Kapu System in later chapters.

Some Christians may say, *"How can the people of Polynesia know the God of the Bible before missionaries brought the Bible?"* It would be un-scriptural if they didn't know the God of the Bible because the Bible says they knew Him. Romans 1:20 NIV says, *"For since the creation of the world God's invisible qualities, his eternal power and divine nature, have been clearly seen, being understood from what has been made, so that people are without excuse."* Acts 17:26-28 says, *"From one man he made all the nations, that they should inhabit the whole earth; and he marked out their appointed times in history and the boundaries of their lands. God did this so that they would seek him and perhaps reach out for him and find him, though he is not far from any one of us. 'For in him we live and move and have our being.' As some of your own poets have said, 'We are his offspring* (creation, not sexually procreated children)." If, since the creation of the world, God's invisible qualities, eternal power and divine nature have been clearly seen so that all people are without excuse to know Him and in God they all lived, moved, had their being and were God's offspring, wouldn't it be likely that there is something about their Creator in their traditions?

# Chapter 3

# Why is the Knowledge of 'Io Not Common in Hawai'i and Polynesia?

A few Hawaiian Historians have revealed their knowledge of 'Io and a few trusted foreign Historians have been entrusted with this knowledge. The oral histories of many mentors, friends and acquaintances of mine, including my own hānai family confirm that a knowledge of 'Io was retained; although sometimes distorted by years of secrecy, veiled language, and mixture with the traditions of other migrations.

One main reason little was written about 'Io is that his knowledge was so holy/sacred. 'Io was either not spoken of or hidden in *kaona* (inner hidden/secret meaning). Hawaiians and Polynesians hid sacred things in plain sight, only the priests with special knowledge knew the *kaona* of the words. Thus, some chants about the 'Io, the Hawaiian hawk (who can see all because he flies so high) and the pueo, Hawaiian owl (because he can see in the darkness and all around) were really chants about the Supreme God

31

without the common people knowing it. This caused some researchers to think there was a bird cult because the *kaona* of the chant was not revealed to them.

Some chants mentioning *'I* (the supreme, highest, best) and *I'o* (the essence, genuine, significant, real, the truth, true worth) also had deeper sacred meaning. More on this later.

## Abraham Fornander

Martha Beckwith, one of the leading authorities on ancient Hawaiian history, said, *"As Malo is our most reliable native source for ancient practices, so Fornander is the leading foreign authority."*[2] Fornander arrived in Hawai'i shortly after the missionaries and realized almost immediately that the missionaries were replacing the Hawaiian culture with their own. Through his wife, an ali'i of Moloka'i, he became appreciative of the beauty of this rapidly dying culture. Kamehameha V saw that Fornander loved the Hawaiian culture and that he had an extensive knowledge of the Hawaiian language. He, therefore, appointed Fornander to *"find the old Hawai'i"* and record it before it was gone. Kamehameha also appointed the future king, *David Kalākaua*, and the future queen, *Lili'uokalani*, his two best scholars, to assist Fornander. Fornander was led by Kalākaua into the back country that was untouched by Western culture. He was taken to the oldest and most knowledgeable kūpuna there. Accompanied by these high ali'i and with Kamehameha's edict, Fornander was allowed to hear sacred traditions of the ancient past that were never recorded before.[3] Fornander learned from these kūpuna, *"Shreds of a purer cult...still preserved, soiled in appearance and obscured in sense by the contact,...yet standing on the traditional records as heirlooms of the past, as witnesses of a better creed.*"[4] He also said that the chants to the ancient Creator God were "...*specimens of the archaic simplicity of the language, hardly intelligible to the present Hawaiians* (mid-1800s)."[5]

## The Pono Ones

The most sacred and precious tradition of the Hawaiian people was of the intensely holy, God above all "*gods.*" The sacred name of 'Io was so holy/sacred it was not to be spoken in common (*noa*) places or to those not chosen. This name was carefully passed down orally only to those who were deemed worthy, the ones who would respect and be pono with the knowledge. These children were called the "*Pono Ones.*" *Pono* meaning "*righteous,*" but intensely more spiritual, full and deep in Hawaiian. Also, only the very highest priestly families knew of his name.

The family whose legacy is recorded in, *God of Light, God of Darkness*, still does not want their family name known. I had dinner recently with "*Moke Iokane,*" the pseudonym I chose for the "*Pono One*" chosen to fulfill the 800-year-old prophecy to restore his family heiau (temple) to the worship of 'Io. At dinner, he again told me how *"furious!"* he was with me for openly talking about 'Io when we first met. His grandfather had taught him about 'Io and told him 'Io was so sacred he was to tell no one. He never told his brothers, cousins or anyone else. His cousin is also a good friend of mine and it was her grandmother who told *"Moke"* about the 800-year-old prophecy he was destined to fulfill, but his cousin, her granddaughter, was told nothing about 'Io.

Another reason little is left of the Knowledge of 'Io was the destruction of the priests of 'Io by the Kahuna Pā'ao who arrived in Hawai'i from Tahiti circa 1100-1300 A.D.

The Hawaiian historian, *Kepelino*, relates that Pā'ao instituted the severe religious observances which built up the power of the chiefs (ali'i) and priests (kāhuna). This occurred during the last period of migration to Hawai'i from Tahiti. He also says that all of the old kāhuna were put to death during this time.[6]

It is easy then to understand why there is only a vague knowledge of the Supreme God left in Hawai'i. The priests of 'Io who would not be corrupted were either killed by the invader, Pā'ao (More on Pā'ao and the religion he brought later), forced to worship in absolute secrecy or flee the islands. The commoners, on the other hand, didn't know the Supreme God's name. The priests of 'Io that remained hid their knowledge of 'Io and passed their knowledge of 'Io to only one child in each generation called *"The Pono One."* They were told to keep this knowledge secret or die because *Pā'ao* would kill any Hawaiian who mentioned the name of their former God, 'Io.

One of my mentors, *Kahu* (Pastor) Ken Kekoa talked about 'Io on his television program in the early '90s. Several persons of Hawaiian ancestry called him afterwards. These people all had similar stories to tell. After hearing Kahu Ken speak of 'Io on the program, they went to their kūpuna and asked them if this was true. These people all got similar answers. They were told, *"Shush! These things are not to be spoken about!"* When Kahu Ken told them, *"Daniel Kikawa is talking about 'Io."* Their reply was, *"We are waiting to see if he will die first."* Apparently, over the 800 years of being told the knowledge of 'Io must be kept secret on pain of death, speaking of 'Io became thought of as a death curse. When I did not die, more and more people began revealing their knowledge of 'Io.

Why am I revealing the name of 'Io now? It is of vital importance to the Hawaiian people today. I do so with the confirmation, permission and support of my Hawaiian 'ohana and mentors. The reasons will be explained in a later chapter.

Another reason will be explained in <u>Chapter 3: Why Do Native Peoples Keep Their Sacred God Secret.</u>

## More Evidence of Secrecy

The Bishop Museum anthropologist, E.S. Craighill Handy, was shown a chant offered to 'Io. It was only shown to him if he promised never to write down its content or even share its content orally. The priests of Polynesia were under strict oath not to tell of the most sacred things, and the penalty for breaking this oath was often death. More on this in a later chapter. Handy said that it is doubtful that the

Lehua Blossoms

common people were even allowed to know the true name of the Supreme Being.[7]

Handy wrote, *"To the question, why has the cult of 'Io not been revealed before, I have only to say that my own studies in spirit-lore, mediumship, hula, therapy, planting, etc., in recent years, have left me amazed at the superficiality of our earlier knowledge of Hawaiian religions. The names 'Io and Uli were already in print, but had never been examined, nor particular inquiry made respecting them, and they were not names on which knowing Hawaiians would volunteer information for reasons shown below."*[8]

Hawaiians hid the sacred in plain sight, only those who knew the kaona of a chant knew what the chant was actually about. For instance, a chant about a fighting chicken was actually about Kamehameha and chants that mentioned *"the lehua has fallen"* are really about the first royal warrior slain in battle. Lehua having the kaona of chiefly blood. These things may be difficult for Western Thinkers to understand.

*Ahu'ena Taylor* was an authority on Hawaiian history, genealogy, and language. In the 1920s, Taylor was appointed to the Hawaiian Historical and Hawaiian Folklore Commissions. Taylor, a descendant of the priests of 'Io, revealed her knowledge of 'Io to Handy. Ahu'ena, born in 1867, learned of 'Io from a manuscript in her mother's possession. This information was passed to her mother by Ahu'ena's grandmother whose father was *Kahaku'i-i-ka-waiea*, who was the *kahuna nui* (high priest) at *Pu'u-o-Mane'o heiau* (temple) in *Honokane*, *Kohala* during the time of Kamehameha. Kahaku'i was one of Kamehameha's tutors. This same information was known to be in the possession of another descendant of Kahaku'i who regarded the information too sacred to publish. This is strong evidence that there was a knowledge of 'Io well before the missionaries arrived and before the arrival of *Captain Cook*. That a precious secret like this could not be kept in a Hawaiian family from a grandmother to her grandchild is demeaning to this family and Hawaiians. I have heard of families keeping recipes secret for longer than this.

According to *Ahu'ena* and her mother *Pu'uheana*, the name of 'Io or 'Iolani was purposely camouflaged by means of pseudonyms to preserve its sanctity.[9] Many of the chants to 'Io that remain are couched in *kaona*. Most Hawaiian words had several layers of meanings ranging from the literal, "*surface*" meaning to layers of kaona. On the surface, many chants to 'Io were outwardly about the owl and the hawk. The owl was symbolic of 'Io because he could see at night. The hawk was the highest flying and most powerful bird in the Hawaiian Islands.

This is not so strange. The owl and the hawk were symbols of 'Io as the lion and lamb are symbols of Jesus.

The God of the Bible is also described as the eagle and a bird who protects its children with its wings. Deut. 32:9-11 NIV says, *"For the Lord's portion is his people, Jacob his allotted inheritance. In a desert land he found him, in a barren and howling waste. He shielded him and cared for him; he guarded him as the apple of his eye, like an eagle that stirs up its nest and covers over its young, that spreads its wings to catch them and carries them aloft."* Psalm 91:4a NIV says, *"He will cover you with his feathers, and under his wings you will find refuge."*

Not only did Hawaiians use much symbolism and many pseudonyms to hide the kaona of a chant but covered it in very *"poetic"* language, synonyms, paraphrases and descriptions.

## Secrecy of The Maori of Aotearoa, New Zealand

I have focused much on the knowledge of 'Io among the Maori because the Maori claim, and their genealogies reflect, that they came from Hawai'i. Hawaiian traditions also reflect why the Maori retained so much of the worship of 'Io. This also will be explained later.

*Sir Peter Buck (Te Rangi Hiroa)*, Director of the Bishop Museum in the early 1990s and professor of anthropology at Yale University, said that the Maori knowledge of 'Io was held by an inner circle of priests who would not impart this knowledge to the uninitiated. The knowledge of 'Io was not known to the general public until the late 1850s when it was revealed by the priest, *Te Matorohanga*. The knowledge of 'Io as the Supreme Being and Creator was confined to the highest order of priests who were called, *tohunga ahurewa.*[10]

In the Bernice P. Bishop Museum, Bulletin 34, Polynesian Religion, C.S.E. Handy writes of the Maori knowledge of 'Io, *"The core of the esoteric theology of the Maori was the concept of the Supreme 'Io which remained wholly unrevealed to foreign enquires for many decades after first contact...I cannot help feeling that our lack of knowledge of such a supreme god in other island groups is due largely to the fact that the knowledge was limited to the ancient priesthood"*[11]

C.O. Davis wrote that, to the Maori priests, to utter the *"ineffable name"* of 'Io under a roof of any kind was to *"blaspheme most frightfully"* and be a sacrilege that only an ignorant person would have the *"depravity"* to attempt.

In the book, *"The Lore of the Whare-wananga"* (the teachings of the Maori sacred House of Learning) translated by S. Percy Smith, President of the Polynesian Society in 1913, Smith records in his preface *"Again, we have in part of the Sage's teaching a story so full of obsolete words and names that the Scribe could not help in the translation, but explained that it was a recitation intended to be delivered to the common people, whilst its true meaning was known only to the priests of old.*

*It may be explained just here that the larger part of the teaching of the Whare-wānanga (or College, house of learning) was never known to the common people—it was too sacred. Especially was the name and all connected with the supreme god 'Io, particularly sacred. His name was never mentioned in the haunts of man. On the few occasions when he was invoked the priests hied* (hid) *them*(selves) *away to the innermost recesses of the forests and there invoked the all powerful supreme god-creator. So that the common people never even heard his name except on some very rare occasions when it entered into*

*one of the invocations—and how rare this was is proved
by the absence of the name in the hundreds of karakias
(prayers, invocations, incantations, etc., etc.) that have
been collected and printed.”* [12]

## Personal Experiences with the Secrecy of ‘Io

Personally, I don't entrust to people I don't know very
well my deepest secrets or information about what is most
precious or valuable to me. I don't blame others for not
wanting to talk with me about ‘Io if they did not know me
well, especially since I am a writer.

A friend from Kaua‘i was talking with a friend of his
from Ni‘ihau. Because he read my book (only *Perpetuated
In Righteousness* at the time) and knew me, he asked his
Ni‘ihauan friend if he knew about ‘Io. His friend told him
he did. When my friend called me and told me that his
Ni‘ihauan friend said he knew about ‘Io, I asked if his
Ni‘ihauan friend would consent to talk with me about ‘Io.
Since my friend knew and trusted me, maybe his friend
would trust me. When my friend gave my request to the
Ni‘ihauan, he shut down right away and would say no
more!

I met a respected kupuna from another branch of the
*Iokane* (a pseudonym) family. When I heard his last name, I
knew he was descended from the priesthood of ‘Io. So, one
day as we were barbecuing outside for our dinner, I asked
him very cautiously, while looking at my grilling, *“Oh,
your last name is Iokane, so you are from the family of the
priesthood of ‘Io.”* Out of the corner of my eye, I saw him
jump a step back with surprise on his face. He looked at me
and slowly and cautiously said, *“Yyyyeeeeaaaahhhhhh.”*
Desiring not to be aggressive, I said as politely as possible,

*"Maybe someday, you can share with me about 'Io."* He replied cautiously, *"Maybe...I was only going to tell my daughter."* We never talked further about 'Io and I never pushed him further about it. I give him my respect for protecting this precious legacy.

When Leon Kāulahao Siu and I first met *Auntie Malia Craver* in 1993 (More background on *Auntie Malia* later) at the Ka'a'awa offices of QLCC (Lili'uokalani Trust), she shared with us about 'Io. After sharing with us for quite a while she said, *"I no usually talk about 'Io,*

Leon Kāulahao Siu

*you know."* Leon and I were confused and just smiled. We had just met her and she had shared so much to us about 'Io. But Auntie is so sharp, without saying a word, she got up and stuck her head into the office across the hall. *"E, How long I know you?"* she said to the person sitting there. *"Eight years, Auntie." "I wen ever tell you about 'Io?" "No, Auntie,"* was the reply. Then she just walked back across the hall and sat down. After getting to know Auntie, I found out what a spiritually insightful and sharp person she was. She had sensed our spirits and confirmed with *Ke Akua* (God), 'Io, it was okay to share. That's why she shared so openly. Several times after that, when we would meet, she would answer the question I was thinking about before I spoke it. This kind of sensitivity to the voice of God was common in the kūpuna of the generation before me. I was blessed to have kūpuna and mentors who were full of Aloha, loved their culture and loved the God of the Bible. I will explain in later chapters why this was such a rare and difficult balance to keep.

# Chapter 4

# Why Do Native Peoples Keep Their Sacred God Secret

The God of the Polynesians was too sacred to be mentioned openly. This was also true of the Israelites' God, Yahweh. This is why the Israelites also called their God by paraphrases and synonyms, like *Elohim* (God Almighty) or *Adonai* (Lord). This is not unusual. The ancient name of the One True God of *Aneityum* (New Hebrides), Nigeria, the *Yezidis* (Turkey), the Incas, the Navaho and other ancient cultures also were not openly mentioned.[13]

This was not an unusual situation. In ancient Babylon at one time, the priests were monotheistic, and the people were polytheistic as it was in Polynesia.[14] This was also the situation with the ancient Chinese, Nigerians, Incas, and other peoples.

The Navajo Indians also never mentioned the name of their One True God to the "*white man.*" Steve Watkins, a friend of Don Richardson (One of my mentors, author and linguist), grew up among the Navajo. He was well

Don Richardson

accepted by them and spoke their language, but he had never heard the Navajo mention the One Creator God. When queried about it by Don, Steve said he was positive that the Navajo never believed in One Creator God. However, urged by Don, he returned to the Four Corners Navajo Reservation to ask the medicine man about it. Steve asked the medicine man if the Navajo had One Creator God and was shocked when the medicine man said *"Yes!"* Hurt, he asked the medicine man why he had never heard the name of this God mentioned even though he had grown up among them and was accepted by them. The medicine man replied that the Navajo elders had gathered together long ago and decided never to reveal the name of their God to the white man. He said that they had decided this because their God was so sacred and precious to them that they could not bear to have the white man belittle, laugh at, ridicule, or call their God the devil. After making him promise not to reveal the name of their precious God, Steve was told the name by the medicine man. True to his promise, Steve has never revealed the name, but the translation of that name he was allowed to share, *"The Glorious One Who Travels Alone."*

Auntie Malia Craver told me that her kūpuna accepted Jehovah but never told the missionaries about ʻĪo because they did not want their precious God to be ridiculed or called the devil. However, she would hear her kūpuna say while praying, *"Jehovah, you are ʻĪo."*

The precious and very sacred name of God and His traditions were not revealed in many native cultures. They were not revealed for the same reason I have held back some of the details of 'Io traditions I have learned. My prayer for what I have revealed in this book is that the name of 'Io and these precious legacies would not be treated the way Auntie Malia and the Navaho feared their most precious God and legacy would be treated.

My Hawaiian kūpuna and mentors confirmed my belief that the Creator wanted His Hawaiian people to know again the name of their true God. I pray that this most sacred God of the Polynesians would not be dishonored or called the devil. I pray that these precious traditions entrusted to me would not be called heathen lies and the good people who entrusted them to me be called liars and exaggerators. This would not only dishonor them, but all their 'ohana and kūpuna. It would not only dishonor me but all my 'ohana and our kūpuna, and my mentors and all their 'ohana and kūpuna. Please, treat these precious people, our 'ohana and kūpuna with Aloha.

# Chapter 5

# Knowledge of 'Īo in Hawai'i

## Written Knowledge of 'Īo in Hawai'i

Written accounts are so important to many in Western academia. There have been a few who have told me my oral sources were not valid. I asked them, *"So, what you are telling me is that the Hawaiian people had no history, culture or religion until the first White Man came and wrote down what he saw?"* They had no answer for me because most accounts of ancient events come from oral sources.

The oldest written mention of 'Īo in Hawai'i that I have found is in the form of *'Ī* . The form of the name that I was taught by Uncle *Bill Kalikolehua Panui* (More on Uncle Bill later). This form of the name was used in a chant composed by *Hewahewa*, the last *Kahuna Nui* (High Priest) of the *Kapu System*, to greet the missionaries in 1820. In line 17 of this chant it says *"Jehovah, 'Ī, ka makemake."*

It is translated into English as, "*Jehovah, the Supreme, our desire.*" But if the kaona of the word "*'I* " is used, this chant says, "*Jehovah, 'I, our desire fulfilled.*" Hewahewa had connected 'Io with Jehovah. One of my main mentors of the knowledge of 'Io, Auntie Malia Craver (More on Auntie Malia below) was a descendant of Hewahewa.

*Abraham Fornander* was chosen by Kamehameha V to find and record the "old Hawai'i" before it was lost. Fornander said, "*...I learn that the ancient Hawaiians at one time believed in and worshipped one god...*" Evidently, he was told of the name of 'Io but, like others, never recorded the name in writing because the name was too sacred. Like the name of the Hebrew God, and of many other peoples, pseudonyms couched in kaona were used because the name was too holy to be spoken. Some of the pseudonyms recorded by Fornander were *Oi-e* signifying *Most Excellent Supreme; Ili-o-mea-lani* meaning *The Reflection of That Chiefly Someone*; *Kue-manu-ai-lehua*, literally *The Beak That Feeds on Lehuas* but meaning *The Power of Death*; *Uli* meaning *Eternity, Beyond Vision* and *Kū-kauhai*, meaning *The One Established*.[15] These names were titles of the One True God, his true name being too sacred to mention.

Mary Kawena Pukui, probably the most respected Hawaiian historian and reservoir of cultural knowledge in modern times, also knew of 'Io but never fully revealed the kaona of the name. Pukui said, "*'Io was referred to as Ili-o-mea-lani* (the reflection of that chiefly someone), *Kū'e-manu-ai-lehua* (the beak that feeds on *lehuas* or the power of death), *and Uli* (eternity, chaos, beyond vision)," some of the pseudonyms mentioned by Fornander for 'Io.[16]

In the book, *The Betrayal of Lili'uokalani* is recorded, *"An old Hawaiian proverb was translated by Kalākaua as 'Beware when you feel you have gained your own peace, for only I'o brings true peace."* The same book records that Lili'uokalani shared the *"views of earlier times,"* among them, the knowledge of 'Io.[17]

As mentioned previously, Abraham Fornander was appointed by King Kamehameha V to *"find the old Hawai'i"* and record it before it was gone. Kamehameha also appointed the future king, *David Kalākaua*, and the future queen, *Lili'uokalani*, his two best scholars, to assist him. Fornander was led by Kalākaua into the back country that was untouched by Western culture to the oldest and most knowledgeable kūpuna. Accompanied by these high ali'i and with Kamehameha's edict, Fornander was allowed to hear sacred traditions of the ancient past that were never recorded before. Therefore, these three— Fornander with the edict of the King and accompanied by two of the best scholars and highest ali'i in Hawai'i, Kalākaua and Lili'uokalani—of any persons in Hawaiian history, should have heard many of the oldest, most sacred and truest traditions of Hawai'i.

As mentioned earlier, Ahu'ena Taylor, an authority on Hawaiian history, genealogy, and language revealed her knowledge of 'Io to E.S.C. Handy, anthropologist for the Bishop Museum.[18]

Ahu'ena learned of 'Io from a manuscript in her mother's possession. This information was passed to her mother by her grandmother whose father was Kahaku'i-i-ka-waiea, who was the kāhuna nui (high priest) at Pu'u-o-Mane'o heiau in Honokane, Kohala during the time of Kamehameha. Kahaku'i was one of Kamehameha's tutors.

Honokane, Kohala

Handy records the following prayer to 'Io. He said that the prayer below was *"first copied.. from a manuscript book belonging to Ahu'ena's mother...Subsequently Ahu'ena graciously consented to go over them very carefully in the Bishop Museum with me alone, giving me permission to use them as and when seemed fitting, with due respect for their sacredness. It is my privilege first to present Ahu'ena's own translations of the two prayers to 'Io, which, as I understand it, she originally planned to include with her article on Iolani but ere going to print decided to withhold."*

*"A PRAYER*
*Translated by Ahu'ena*

*"Oh 'Io! Oh 'Io!*
*A proclamation to the house-top by thy man-servant.*
*No other god can ascend*
*Thy mountainous tabu,*

*Thou art 'Iolani, the eyes of graceful eternity—*
*Eternity who watches the unrighteous,*
*Eternity who watches the righteous.*
*Have pity on thy offspring,*
*Guard him from all misfortunes that might befall*
*him,*
*Look thou upon*
*The one who is doing evil to me,*
*Forever and ever*
*Amen.—The prayer is free."*

*Ahu'ena describes a 'priesthood of 'Io,' quot-*
*ing directly from her mother's note book as fol-*
*lows: "The Priesthood of Iolani was the highest*
*priesthood of the islands of Hawaii. Neither*
*chieftains nor priests dared utter the word 'Io for*
*fear that Po and Uli would bite or punish them.*
*'Io is the Holy Spirit, the invisible someone; its*
*only symbol on earth is the young owl with eyes*
*that see at night. There was no human sacrifice*
*on this altar. The priests killed or saved life with*
*prayers by calling to 'Io to adjust all wrong. The*
*people by this religious order did believe, how-*
*ever, in stoning a wrong-doer to death. The priests*
*of 'Io were feared and respected and were called*
*the order of Wahamana and Ha-mana (powerful*
*lips and breath of power). KeAli'imaika'i was an*
*Ali'i Kapu Akua of 'Io. 'Io to us is Jehovah to*
*other peoples.*[19]

This statement clearly shows that Ahu'ena's family
did connect 'Io to the God of the Bible as did many other

51

families. Although there were no human sacrifices to ʻĪo, there was still a fearful, very reverent *"Old Testament-like,"* protocol to approach such a powerful and holy God. The Hebrew people were also so much in fear and reverence of their holy God that they didn't mention the name of *Yahweh* (Jehovah) either. Again, this is one main reason little is retained about ʻĪo. We will see this among the Maori as well.

Truly, it was with great trepidation that I began openly sharing about ʻĪo. If I wasn't so convicted that this was God's will for this time and with the encouragement, support and confirmation of my kūpuna and mentors; I would not have done it.

As mentioned earlier, it was recorded of the Maori God, ʻĪo, *"…the common people never even heard his name except on some very rare occasions when it entered into one of the invocations—and how rare this was is proved by the absence of the name in the hundreds of karakias (prayers, invocations, incantations, etc., etc.) that have been collected and printed."* [20] When the name entered a

David Malo

chant, what it meant was not known to the common people.

The respected Hawaiian historian, David Malo, recorded such a rare instance in a chant that is regaining popularity today called, *"Hemu Oia."* The chant closes with "ʻĪa E!" (Oh ʻĪa!) ʻĪa being a dialect of the name, ʻĪo.[21]

In *Nā Inoa Hōkū, A Catalogue of Hawaiian and Pacific Star Names*, the North Star is called in Hawaiian, *Hōkū Pa'a* (signifying: The Star that Does Not Move). The North Star is the only star in the sky that does not move. All the other stars of the heavens revolve around it. It is the center of the heavens. Two ancient Polynesian names for this star were: *Kio Pa'a*[22] and *'Io Pa'a*, 'Io the immovable/steadfast/unchanging. It was also known simply as *Kio* (Southern Polynesian dialect for 'Io) or *Kioio*.[23]

It is claimed about Kaua'i on the website mauiculture.net, "*Just below the crest of Mount Kawaikini* (the highest point on Kaua'i) *stood the holiest of the holy, the sacred Heiau of the Supreme 'Io - the only temple outside of the island of Hawai'i erected to honor 'Io.*"[24] I have found information of other 'Io heiaus on O'ahu, Maui and Moloka'i.

## Oral Sources of 'Io in Hawai'i

I have 38 oral sources for 'Io in Hawai'i. Some of whom are listed below.

My three main mentors about 'Io were:

*Auntie Malia Kawaiho Ouluoha'ao Craver*. Auntie Malia was a descendant of Hewahewa (the last kahuna nui of the Kapu System) and the protégé of *Mary*

*Kawena Pukui*. Auntie Malia received the *Order of Ke Aliʻi Pauahi*, the *David Malo Award* and was selected in 2007 as a *Living Treasure*. She was asked to explain the Hawaiian method of reconciliation, *hoʻoponopono*, to the joint session of the United Nations and was the cultural and spiritual advisor for the *Queen Liliʻuokalani Children's Center* (now the Liliʻuokalani Trust). Auntie Malia told me that, when she was young, growing up in *Hoʻokena* (one of the last traditional Hawaiian fishing villages and a favorite retreat of Queen Liliʻuokalani), when she would go fishing with her uncles, they would pray to ʻIo with every paddle. When she would go with her kūpuna planting, they would pray to ʻIo with each seed or huli they planted. Auntie Malia told me that although her kūpuna worshipped the Supreme Being, ʻIo, daily and taught her to do the same, they rarely mentioned their belief in ʻIo to those outside of the ʻohana. Until she died, Auntie Malia did not speak of ʻIo unless asked specifically about ʻIo and only if she could see that the person would respect this knowledge and not belittle her God. She said that when Christianity came to Hawaiʻi, there was confusion in the ʻohana because they already had a Supreme Being. The last Kahuna Nui of the Kapu System, Hewahewa Nui, was her ancestor who met the missionaries. In an interview in the *ʻIolani* Newspaper, Auntie Malia related that her ancestors said, "*Let us go to this church and listen to their minister. If it is good and they are right in their teaching about their powerful God of the universe, then we will keep that same God. The reason is that we have a God like theirs. If they are exaggerating that their God is better than our God, then they are wrong. We Hawaiians have had a powerful and all-knowing God from the beginning and until today.*"[25] Her kūpuna accepted Jehovah but never told the missionaries about 'Io because they knew that their God would be ridiculed and called the devil by the missionaries. However, she would hear her kūpuna say while pray-ing, *"Jehovah, you are 'Io."*

My hānai family, also knew of 'Io. Mom Eaton, would tell me, *"We Hawaiians always knew there was only One God."*

Arlene Eaton

From the Midweek newspaper: "*Arlene Wainaha Ku'uleialoha Brede Eaton was honored Sept. 14 with the Kalani Ali'i Award by the Royal Order of Kamehameha I, the Ahahui Ka'ahumanu, Hale O Ali'i O Hawai'i and the Daughters and Sons of The Hawaiian Warriors. 'She is definitely the type of Native Hawaiian leader that we need and who I absolutely look up to,' said Alicia Maluafiti, board treasurer of the foun-dation. I hope I can be one-10th as honorable as she is 45 years from now when I am her age.' That won't be an easy goal to achieve, as Eaton has made it her business to spread her culture and history, according to Maluafiti. 'These awards are not given frivolously. There is a lot of discussion that goes about who to honor, who to show respect for, and that's why I think Aunty Arlene not only is deserving of these types of awards ... they give her honor.*"[26]

It was my hānai brother, *Cleighton Ku'ualohaokalaniakea Eaton*, who first revealed 'Io to me as "*'Iaonālaninuiamamao* ('Ia, a dialect of 'Io, of the Great and Distant Heavens)."

55

Both Auntie Malia and Mom Eaton taught me about 'Io as the pinnacle of the "*Lōkahi Triangle*." What is the "*Lōkahi Triangle*?" *Lōkahi* is translated into English as "*Unity;*" however, the Hawaiian is much deeper than that. It is when everything is in perfect harmony and balance; all is Pono and Aloha in heaven and on earth. The *Lōkahi* Triangle is an equilateral triangle with 'Io, Ke Akua, God at the top center of the triangle. One bottom corner is "*Nā Kānaka*," people. The other bottom corner is "*Ka 'Āina*," creation/nature; which is the earth, ocean, atmosphere and all the plants and animals in it. Only when everything is in perfect harmony between the three parts of the triangle, which necessitates all being Pono and filled with Aloha; can there be true Lōkahi. First we must be in harmony, Pono and Aloha with Ke Akua, 'Io, God. We must then be in harmony, Pono and Aloha with all people. Again, you can hate what people do but you must Aloha and be Pono

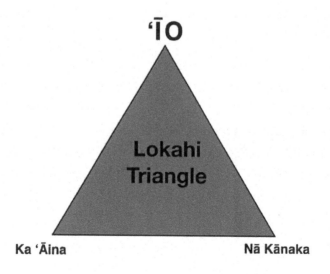

with them. Then we must be in harmony with creation/nature. 'Io made men and women in His image. He made them "Nā Kahu," Caretakers of His creation. Ka Bibala, the Bible, says that the invisible God can be clearly seen in His creation. That we can even learn of His eternal power and character from creation (Rom. 1:20). Therefore, we should treat Ka 'Āina/creation with great respect as we are its Nā Kahu/Caretakers entrusted by 'Io/Ke Akua/God with its care. We need to be Pono with and "Aloha 'Āina."

*William Kalikolehua Pānui* taught me that he knew of 'Io simply as *'I*. Uncle Bill's maternal grandfather and *hānai father, Tūtū Kaua*, was a well-known historian of the *Ke'ei-Nāpo'opo'o* region and an authority on a wide range of cultural matters. Tūtū Kaua was  born at Ke'ei in 1863 and was often sought out on matters of Hawaiian history, until his passing in 1960, at the age 97. Uncle Bill, a gifted story teller would freely share his recollections of histories, families and sites of *Ke'ei* and neighboring lands. He won the *Nā Hōkū Hanohano "Haku Mele"* award in 1993 for the song, *"Ke Alaula."*

Uncle Bill told me that he knew 'Io simply as *'I*. He explained that the surface meaning of 'I is the Supreme, but the kaona meaning is the Supreme Being. The suffix *– o* ("*of*" as in 'I-o) connoted "*of all*," *The Supreme One Of All*. I will always be humbled that Uncle Bill drove with Auntie Namahana to Hilo from their home in Ke'ei

(between Kealakekua Bay and Pu'uhonua 'O Honaunau)
specifically to share his knowledge with me for two
days. He shared with me about 'Ī and then showed me an
issue of *Ke Ola* magazine that honored a respected cultural practitioner and historian, *David Kahelemauna Roy*
(deceased). The article states, "*A Kahu holds a kulana
(station) with a kuleana (responsibility) to Ka 'Ī (Divine
Creator)...Residents of Hawaii are all seated in the cradle
of transformation-a fireplace in the Home of Ka 'Ī-lala-
'ole (Supreme-One-Without-Branches)*"[27] Then he showed
me the second listed meaning of 'Ī in Pukui's Hawaiian
Dictionary which says in part, "*(frequently a part of
names, as Ka 'Ī-i-mamao, the supreme one at a distance:
'Ī-lala-'ole, supreme without branches.*" Although Pukui
only listed the surface meaning of 'Ī, she revealed that
she knew of 'Io to those who understood the kaona of
the name because she lists several names of the Supreme
God, 'Ī. One is *Ka 'Ī-lala-'ole* "*Supreme One Without
Branches*" (*The Supreme God Without Descendants*). This
goes with another name of 'Io, *'Io-Makua-'Ole* (*Supreme
God Without Parents*). All the other gods had parents and
descendants. Pukui also mentions, *Ka'Ī-i-mamao* (*The
Supreme One at a Distance*) which is like another name
for 'Io, *'Ia-'O-Nā-Lani-Nui-A-Mamao*, *'Ia of the Great
and Distant Heavens*.

These three main mentors of mine in the knowledge
of 'Io, Auntie Malia, Mom Eaton and Uncle Bill, were all
very respected native speakers (manaleo) brought up in
their culture. These three primary sources alone give for-
midable credibility of the knowledge of 'Io in Hawai'i.

I also spent much time talking with the eldest kupuna
of the Iokane family about 'Io and with the "*Pono One*"

of the family, *Moke* (a pseudonym). Moke fulfilled the 800-year-old prophecy of 'Io written about in the book, *God of Light, God of Darkness*. Moke told me his grandfather taught him about 'Io by using the 'Io, the Hawaiian hawk, as an example. His grandfather would tell him, "*See how the 'Io flies so high in the sky. From his perch in the sky, he can see the clouds being blown against the mountains and falling as rain. He can see the raindrops form rivulets and then streams that become rivers that empty into the vast ocean. So 'Io can see the stream of your life from beginning to end.*" More about *God of Light, God of Darkness* in another chapter.

Mickey Ioane, is the writer and composer of the song, Hawai'i '78, one of the top 50 songs in Hawaiian music history. Mickey gave the song to his friend, Israel Kamakawiwo'ole (IZ), to record. Mickey's grandfather had taught him about 'Io. We have had long conversations about 'Io together.

Kahu Kihapi'ilani (Kiha) Pimental was told by his great grandmother, Laurita Lae'ole, a manaleo (native speaker), that the Hawaiian people always believed in One True God, 'Io. She made him promise only to pray to 'Io-Lani and to pray for her. He was 10-years-old at the time, she never brought it up again. He did not hear anyone speak of 'Io again until the summer after 7th grade when Kamehameha School Dorm Advisor, Tim Bowden, told him the same thing. He said our people always believed in One True God, 'Io. He was greater than all the lesser gods including Pele, Kane, Lono, Ku and Kanaloa.

One of the co-founders of *Aloha Ke Akua* is *Kawika Kahiapo*. Kawika was awarded a Lifetime Achievement award for Slack Key Guitar as well as multiple *Nā Hōkū*

*Hanohano* awards. Kawika was asked to play music for the opening of a park. The park was being given to the community from a private foundation. The park is within an ancient *ahupua'a* (pie shaped Hawaiian subdivision of land from the mountain to the sea). The elder kupuna of the Hawaiian family whose ahupua'a it was, was also invited. When he saw Kawika he said, *"E, secret's out, e."* Kawika replied, *"Huh?* "Secret's out, *e."* *"Huh?"* *"Secret's out, e."* *"What do you mean?"* *"You da one sing, 'O 'Oe 'Io, right?"* *"Yea."* *"Secret's out, e."* This kupuna's family also knew of 'Io but like all the families of 'Io, it had been kept secret.

The song, *'O 'Oe 'Io*, was written at a Native Songwriters Retreat I organized for Aloha Ke Akua. 'O 'Oe 'Io was originally written as *Ko Koe 'Io* (okinas are "Ks" for most Maori words) by two Maori, *Luke Kaa Morgan* and *Dale Garratt*. It was translated into Hawaiian at the retreat by Kumu Hula *Kaho'okele Crabbe*. Kawika Kahiapo, who sings this song on the *Na Kahu* and *Kaukahi*

CDs, has had many people tell him how much this song has meant to them. It has touched the Hawaiian soul/na'au in a deep way. One well known Hawaiian music artist told Kawika, "*I just play this song over and over, I press repeat, repeat, repeat.*" Another cultural practitioner told Kawika, "*When I first heard this song, it touched me so deeply I had to pull over on the side of the road. I couldn't drive.*"

One kupuna and an Elder in a Hawaiian Church told me, "*If you haven't heard this song, you have never been in a Hawaiian Church!*" It is being sung and danced at weddings, funerals, community events, canoe races and more. 'O 'Oe 'Io has been sung and danced at the Vatican twice, for the canonizations of Father Damien and Sister Marianne Cope. Why would this song touch the hearts of Hawaiians so deeply if there was not the hidden remembrance of this One Benevolent Creator God?

*Kaho'okele Crabbe*

# O OE 'Io

**'O 'Oe 'Io, E Makualani**
*You are 'Io, Heavenly Father*

**'O 'Oe 'Io, Ka Waiola**
*You are 'Io, the Living Water*

**'O 'Oe 'Io, E Kumu Ola**
*You are 'Io, the Source of Life*

**Ka mea hana i nā mea a pau**
*The one who has made all things*

**E Ku'u Haku, Ka Mauna Ki'eki'e**
*My Lord who is the Highest Mountain*

**'O 'Oe 'Io**

# Maori

**Ko Koe 'Io, Matua te kore**
*You are 'Io, the Self Existent One*

**Ko koe 'Io, Te waiora**
*You are 'Io, the Source of Life*

**Ko Koe 'Io, Te pukenga**
*You are 'Io, The Source*

**Te kaihanga o nga mea katoa**
*The Creator of all things*

**Ko koe te toka, te mauna keikei**
*You are the Rock, the Highest Mountain*

**Ko koe 'Io**

Kawika composed the music for He Waiwai Nui written by his cousin Lehua Kawaikapuokalani Hewitt. The song is about how the "Water of Life" must flow from Heaven to our Kūpuna and to the next generation for future generations to be healthy. The chorus of the song says, "Ola ka Hā (Life from the Spirit of God), Ola ka Wai (Life from the Water of Life, Iesū), Ola ka 'Ī (Life from the Supreme God, 'Io)." This is, Ha-Wai-'Ī, the name of the `aina that 'Io gave our people to kahu (be caretakers of). We need to return to our true God of Aloha so the Living Water will again flow freely."

A Hawaiian friend who married a Maori man told me after I shared with them what I knew of 'Io that she also knew of 'Io, as did her Maori husband. She said to me, however, that she felt she needed to repent. I asked her why. She told me in shame that she had found an old genealogy in her aunt's closet. In the genealogy, it said her family were priests of 'Io. When Pā'ao came and gave the priests of 'Io the three choices: (1)Resist and die (The Hawaiian historian *Kepelino* wrote that "*all the priests of the old religion were killed*"), (2) join him and keep your priestly rank (But now you must worship his gods and do human sacrifices on the sacred heiau to 'Io, to whom man was sacred and not to be killed), or (3) step down from your priestly rank, become a lowly maka'āinana and never speak of 'Io again (This last group passed the knowledge of 'Io in secret to one child in each generation, the *Pono One*, on pain of death); her family had chosen the second choice and joined Pā'ao. More on this later.

Respected Maui kupuna and cultural practitioner, *Charlie Kauluwehi Maxwell* (deceased), knew of 'Io. He came to a talk that I was giving on Maui and spoke with me afterwards. He said he came to refute me but found that he agreed with everything I said and we became friends.

*Don Kealoha Ahia* (deceased) was the first of several kūpuna who told me they learned of 'Io from their kūpuna in this way; "*Ha-The Breath of Life (The Holy Spirit), Wai-The Water of Life (Iesū, Jesus),* and *'Ī -short for 'Io (the Supreme Being).*" Here we have the triune Creator God in the very name of Hawai'i.

I was speaking to a class about 'Io when a woman said angrily, "*But what about those who were not the Pono One? What about them!*" I saw that she was angry but couldn't understand why. After the class, I asked her, "*I see that you are upset about something, can you explain to me about your statement?*" She replied that she had read my book (This was only *Perpetuated In Righteousness* at this time) and asked her parents if their family knew of 'Io. They replied they did. She then asked why she was not told. Their reply was, "*Because you were not the Pono One, your sister was.*" She then went to ask her sister to share with her about 'Io. Her sister refused. I could then understand why she was so angry.

Respected Native speaker, cultural practitioner and historian Akoni Akana (deceased) said that Hawaiians believed in a multitude of gods. He also said, however, that his great grandmother taught him about 'Io, that 'Io is the Light and the absolute Truth of All.

*Kahu* (Pastor) *John Trusdell,* also a descendant of Hewahewa, but who did not know Auntie Malia, told me that in the 1970s, he would go to his grand aunt's house after school in Kalihi, O'ahu. She would tell him about their God, 'Io. Much later, as a Big Island Kahu, he would also take fish and poi to a kupuna in the *Pana'ewa* Hawaiian Homestead. She would share with him about 'Io also.

*Kahu Greg Dela Cruz* was speaking to a Hawaiian Civic Group in San Diego. He asked them, *"How many of you have heard your kūpuna whisper about 'Io?"* Six people raised their hands.

When I spoke at Glad Tidings Church, *Curtis Malia* came up to me afterwards and told me his uncle *Jonah Aweau* told him about 'Io. His uncle said that he would teach Curtis about 'Io but passed away before he could.

Kaleo Haleakalā told me that his grandmother ended all her prayers with *"'Ia E!"* (*Oh 'Ia!*). 'Ia being a dialect of 'Io. As mentioned previously, the historian David Malo, recorded a chant that ended with *"'Ia E!"*

It was told to me that there was an ancient heiau dedicated to 'Io on the top of *Kauiki* Head, Hana, Maui. This makes sense since it is the traditional birthplace of *Hema*, who Ahu'ena Taylor says was a priest of 'Io and discoverer of Aotearoa (New Zealand). The Hawaiian historian, *Kamakau*, also says that Hema discovered Aotearoa. When my Hānai brother, Ākea Eaton, was living on Maui,

Kauiki Head Hana, Maui

he was told by his cousin that in the 1970's a tohunga from Aotearoa found the sacred places of his ancestor, Hema, in Hana by his genealogy chant. Hema is also in the genealogy chant of the first Maori King, Potatau.

*Kahu Liefy Ha'o* also shared with me about 'Io. She is related to *Papa Auwai* (deceased), who was one of the most respected *Kahuna La'au Lapa'au* (herbal healer). Papa Auwai also knew of 'Io.

Mana'oi'o, means Faith. Mana means Spiritual Power, i'o means True and the kaona is 'Io, the Absolute Truth of All. Faith is the Spiritual Power that comes from 'Io.

'Iao Valley, Maui

Another kupuna told me that 'Iao Valley on Maui was dedicated to 'Io. Hema is said to be buried there. 'I-ao – *"The Supreme God of Light."*

Kupuna *Leona Toler* (deceased) of *Keaukaha* Hawaiian Homestead, Hilo shared that, as the Pono One for her family, her grandmother taught her about 'Io.

# Chapter 6

# The Knowledge of 'Io in Other Polynesian Islands

## Aotearoa (New Zealand)

The knowledge of 'Io has been uncovered in a majority of Maori tribes. This is considerable when one realizes that most priests of 'Io believed revealing this knowledge meant death.[28] I have found over 20 written sources from New Zealand that mention 'Io. Some of them are the oldest written records of the Maori.

The first king of the Maori, Potatau Te Wherowhero and his son, the second king, Tawhiao, were both high priests of the 'Io religion. There is no one today of that rank. The book *King Potatau* contains a genealogy of the King that goes back to the three famous navigators and priests of 'Io from Hawai'i, 'Aikanaka (Kaitangata-Maori dialect), Hema (Hema-Maori), and Kaha'i (Tawhaki-Maori dialect). King Potatau was chosen as king because he had whakapapa (genealogy) back to seven of the major canoes the Maori came to Aotearoa on. Most of those seven have the knowledge of 'Io (Tainui, Takitimu, Te Arawa, Matatua, Aotea, Kurahaupō that I know of). More on these two kings in a later chapter.

The Rev. and Nga Puhi elder, Maori Marsden's (1924-1993) great grandfather was a priest of the 'Io religion. His great grandfather was born in 1790.[29] He was a priest of 'Io before the first missionaries arrived in 1814. Maori Marsden was a Maori scholar, writer, Christian pastor and also traditional Tohunga. He was trained at the *Tai Tokerau Te Aupouri* Ware Wananga and wrote of 'Io.

In 1833, Judge Manning was the only white man initiated into the priesthood of 'Io. 'Io priests were not allowed to share the knowledge of 'Io outside of the Whare Wananga. He wrote a manuscript about the precepts and religion of 'Io. However, before he died, he was convicted of his oath and burned it.[30]

In 1842, French missionary, Catherin Servant, knew of the belief in 'Io among the Maori.[31]

In 1852, the Rev. Richard Taylor writes, "*'Io, the great God of Waikato and Ngati Kahungunu. The resemblance of His name to Ihowa was pointed out to me by the natives themselves, who still affirm it to be the ancient name of this God. They say He was the Maker of heaven and earth and the first man.*"[32]

In his *Life and Times of Patuone* (a Nga Puhi Chief), published in 1876, C. O. Davis writes: "*I have been informed by natives well acquainted with the ancient mode of worship among their people that the oldest Maori prayers were those addressed to the sacred Io. The following lines from a primitive recitation refer to this great deity:—*

*Nekea, e Whakatau, ki runga o Hawaiki*

*Whakaturia to whare, me ko te maru a Io"*
This is rendered by Davis as — *"Move on, O Whakatau, move to Hawaiki* (Hawai'i – Maori dialect). *Establish there thy house, as though it were under the protecting care of Io."*[33]

Elsdon Best writes that the number of men initiated in the knowledge of 'Io was small and the common people knew no part of it and maybe only rarely heard the name. He writes in vol. 3 of the *Memoirs of the Polynesian Society.* *"Some of these have been obtained by the writer, while others are preserved in manuscript books in the possession of natives, which will probably never all be permanently recorded. All this matter is couched in exceedingly archaic language, and it is impossible to believe that it has all been composed during late years* (late years--early 1900s)." [34]

Recorded in the book, *The Lore of the Whare-wananga* translated by S. Percy Smith, President of the Polynesian Society in 1913, *"It will possibly be thought that the idea of Io as the one supreme god creator of all things, is derived from the Christian teachers of the Maori people, and that it has been engrafted on to Maori beliefs in modern times since Christianity was introduced. But I am assured not only by the positive statement of the Scribe, but by internal evidence—more particularly perhaps by the prayers to Io, which contain so many obsolete words, and differ a good deal in form of composition from ordinary karakias* (prayers)—*that there is no foundation for such an idea. The doctrine of Io is evidently a bona-fide relic of very ancient times, handed down with scrupulous care generation after generation, as the centre and core of the esoteric teaching of the Whare-wānanga."* [35]

Heretanunga Pat Baker, author of the thinly veiled historical novel, *Behind The Tattooed Face*, revealed much about the 'Io priesthood, its history and rituals.

The book *Tohunga* records that no idol or image was made of 'Io because 'Io is beyond form or thought.[36] The author, Samuel Timoti Robinson, learned of 'Io from his uncle who in turn learned of 'Io from two very old Tohunga (kāhuna) of his time who learned of 'Io from their elders taking the 'Io knowledge back into the 1700s. He says any thought of an invented 'Io knowledge is inconceivable. He was told that the 'Io tradition came from Hawaiki (Hawai'i). The priests of the 'Io tradition *"proclaim that there is only one Almighty Power, who is the singular creative and sustaining force of the universe.'*[37] *'Io planned for the universe to operate in oneness with the Law of Truth. In accordance with Truth we must progressively manifest good to be in oneness with 'Io. Truth was the most important factor in the 'Io religion. As co-workers of 'Io, we, like the atua* (spiritual beings), *are here to fulfil the divine plan…Not to become obedient slaves of 'Io, nor to be helpless children of some god…this is why we are given the power of choice…to cooperate with 'Io's plan or go against it…that is why we find evil in the world."*[38]

## Personal experiences with the Maori belief in 'Io

I have been to Aotearoa 12 times and have personally met and talked with over 25 kaumatua (Maori Elders) in Aotearoa who held knowledge of 'Io. The knowledge of 'Io was brought to Aotearoa in many of their canoes (*Aotea, Mataatua, Te Arawa, Takitimu, Tainui, Kurahaupo, Mamari, Ngatokimatawhaorua*, to name some). There is more about 'Io in Aotearoa than in any of the other Polynesian Islands. The Maori traditionally came from Hawaiki (Hawai'i).

My hānai brother, Cleighton Ku'ualohaokalaniakea Eaton, told me about a Maori Tohunaga that found the sacred places of our common ancestor, Hema, in Hana, Maui by his genealogy chant.

*Wallace Wihongi* (deceased), a respected *Nga Puhi* (A Maori tribe) *Kaumatua* taught many about the traditions of 'Io and the Nga Puhi connections to Hawaiki. He found places in his genealogy chant near *Ka Lae* Point (South Point, southernmost point in Hawai'i and the traditional leaving point of the Maori) on the Big Island (Hawai'i). His family continues his legacy. We were hosted by *Paul Wihongi* and his whanau (family) at *Te Iringa Marae*, *Kaikohe*, Aotearoa in July 2019.

Nga Puhi Kaumatua, *Peneamine Werohia*, gave me an ancient chant that speaks about a Maori man returning to Hawaiki to marry a Hawaiian cousin. This chant says in part, *"As I, like the godly Tawhaki* (Kaha'i – Hawaiian, famous hero navigator, son of 'Io priest Hema who Ahuena Taylor and Kamakau says discovered Aotearoa, New Zealand, and is the ancestor of both many Maori and Hawaiians)

Peneamine Werohia and Kaleo Waipa
Whangarei, Aotearoa

*am borne along to be landed on the mountain ranges of Hawaiki...There I may view the fires volcanic flaming over Maunga Roa* (Mauna Loa – Hawaiian)...*Since the days of Mawete* (Maweke – Hawaiian, famous Hawaiian ancestor)...*And the fragrance is wafted hither from the hala trees, in these forests of the Fatherland. There I may recline me against the palms which stand at Kowhara* (Kohala-Hawaiian)...*A desire wells within me to take in marriage my tuahine* (kuahine-Hawaiian, female cousin)." *Peneamine*, a respected carver, carved a monument dedicated to 'Io for the *Whangarei* (Hanalei in Hawaiian dialect) Library.

*Dr. Cathy Moana Dewes*, Principal of *Te Kura Kaupapa Maori O Ruamata*, one of the most respected Maori language schools, brought 233 of her students, teachers and care-givers to Hawai'i; the main reason being to see where their ancestors left for Aotearoa. She reported, *"We've retraced the footsteps of our ancestors... We've been to Rarotonga, we've been to Tahiti, we've been to Rangiātea...We went back to the place that our canoe* (This is the *Te Arawa* canoe) *left from and came to Aotearoa from."* I took them on a tour of

Ray Totorewa, Ka Lae Point, Big Island, Hawai'i

historic sites in Ka Lae (South Point, Big Island), traditional point of departure of the Maori to Aotearoa. The students and staff came from different tribes (Iwi) and canoes (Maori can trace themselves back to the canoe their ancestors came on). They were all believers in 'Io.

I took the *Te Kura Kaupapa Maori O Otepou* (Maori language school) staff and students to Ka Lae, South Point. They also knew of 'Io. The two main canoes they came from are Mataatua and Takitimu.

I have taken more than 10 Maori schools and groups to Ka Lae to see where their ancestors left Hawai'i.

Respected Maori educator, politician and Christian leader, *Monte Ohia* (deceased), had the knowledge of 'Io passed on to him through his family. We spent much time talking together about 'Io.

*Graham Cruickshank*, Founder and Principal of International Bible College in Whangarei, New Zealand and I have had much correspondence about the history and traditions of 'Io. His book, *'Io Origins*, confirms many of my sources, both written and oral, as well as new sources. His wife, Tui's, tribe, Nga Puhi, has a strong 'Io tradition.[39]

Respected *Ngati Torehina* (A sub-tribe of Nga Puhi) kaumatua, Te Hurihanga Rihari, shared with me about their tribe's relationship with 'Io.

Long-time friend and author of the book, *He Purapura Ruia – Ranginui Whare Whakairo*, respected *Ngati Ranginui* (Takitimu, Mataatua, Te Arawa) kaumatua and carver, *Huikakahu Kawe*, shared with me about the Takitimu traditions of 'Io.

Charlie Matthews

My hānai Maori brother, Tuhoe tribe kaumatua and historian, Charlie Matthews (deceased), and I shared our knowledge of 'Io together over many years and many hours. I miss our times together dearly.

## Tahiti/Society Islands

*Elsdon Best* recorded that ancient prayers to 'Io were also made by the Tahitians and Rarotongans "...*which disposes of the idea of a modern local* (New Zealand) *invention. Collusion is out of the question.*"[40]

In Tahiti a chant about 'Io begins, "*In the beginning there was nothing but the god Ihoiho...*" *Iho* in the Tahitian means "*the core*," therefore, *Ihoiho* signifies the "*core of cores*" or the very source, the center of existence.

In the Journal of the Polynesian Society, vol. 26, Best also stated about Tahiti, "*Perhaps the most interesting item of information obtained from these natives was the statement made by one man that the principal atua or god of their local pantheon in past times was known as 'Io i te vahi naro ('Io of the hidden place), with which name may be compared that of 'Io mata ngaro ('Io of the hidden face), the supreme god of the Maori folk of New Zealand.*" This would not be unusual because many of the canoes whose common ancestor was Hema went through Tahiti and Rarotonga to Aotearoa.

When *Kahu Hanalei Coleado* was in Tahiti, he spoke with the person who was next in line to be *Tahuʻa Nui* (Kahuna Nui, High Priest) of *Taputapuatea* Marae (Heiau), the most sacred heiau in Polynesia. However, this person refused to take the role of Tahuʻa Nui because *'Oro* (The son of *Taʻaroa* and a god who demands human sacrifices) was now the god of the marae. He told Kahu Hanalei that the original God of the marae was 'Io.

## Rarotonga (Cook Islands)

In Rarotonga, iʻo means pith or core, often with the connotation of god.

In Vol. 19 of the *Journal of the Polynesian Society* appears a translation of the Rarotongan version of the tradition of Rata. It contains the following statement made by a native: "*I may say the god Io was an atua mekameka (beneficent deity), and the ancient priests, my ancestors, always ended up the special karakia (ritual) with this chant: Io, Io, te atua nui ki te rangi tuatinitini ('Io, the great god of the vast heavens).*"[41] We can compare this to the name of 'Io that my hānai brother, Ākea Eaton, taught me, "*'Ia-o-nālani-nui-a-mamao,*" 'Io of the great and distant heavens.

## Tuamotus

The *Tuamotuans* (The *Tuamotus* are an island chain east of Tahiti) also had a hidden high God called *Kiho*. The creation chants of *Kiho* are almost a duplicate of the Maori creation chants of 'Io. *J.F. Stimson* collected the oldest knowledge of 'Io in the Tuamotus. His source was *Fariua-a-Makitaua*, who was taught of 'Io by his grandfather and corroborated in full by *Kamake-a Ituragi*, a celebrated *Fagatau* (elder/priest). Fariua called this god, "*Kiho*" (In much of Southern Polynesia, the "K" replaces the Hawaiian okina so 'Io would be pronounced Kiho or Kio).

In Bulletin 111 of the Bernice P. Bishop Museum, *The Cult of Kiho-tumu*, copyrighted in 1933, Stimson writes, "*These chants of Fariua's (Kiho chants) have been shown to leading sages from many sections of the Tuamotus, and all have expressed the unqualified opinion that they are genuine archaic compositions impossible of imitation in these days* (early 1900s) *when the ancient modes of expression and even the meanings of the words themselves have become widely forgotten and often corrupted by the invading and now nearly universal Tahitian language. It is unlikely that there is a Tuomotuan native alive today capable of composing these, or similar, cosmogonic chants.*"[42]

Stimson compares the nature and character of Kiho worship to the Maori 'Io worship: No sacrifices were made to Kiho/'Io, no images of Kiho/'Io were constructed, worship of Kiho/'Io was limited to the nobility, the religion of Kiho/'Io had nothing in common with black magic.

Stimson believed that the knowledge of Kiho, the Supreme God, was from an early ethnic wave of Polynesians whom he called, *palae-Polynesian*. This knowledge was only taught to the priests and nobles.

## Samoa

IOA LO MĀTOU ATUA/MATUA I LE LAGI TEA.
IOA OUR ORIGIN IN THE PURE/WHITE HEAVENS

By Tagaloa Lupematasila Vaeluagaomatagi Elisara Sao Filioalii, in consultation with chief Misa Telei'ai of Falelatai/Sāmatau 'Upolu Sāmoa and chief Matuāvao Tualāina Meafua of Sāle'aula Sāvaii Sāmoa.

"I am Tagaloa Lupematasila Vaeluagaomatagi Elisara Filioalii, a descendant of King, Alii Tuia'ana Faumuinā, and the ancient King, Alii Tagaloa of Manu'a American Sāmoa and Sāmoa. I hold the Alii title, Tagaloa Lupematasila, on Upolu Island and am the rightful heir to the title King Va'afusu'aga on Savai'i islands of Sāmoa.

Tatalo/lotu:

IOA lo matou matua/Atua i le lagi. E a 'oe le vā nimo, 'o 'oe e ona le vā tea, o oe fo'i na faia le moana ma fanua, le lagi ma le lalolagi 'ātoa. O 'oe o le matā'isau o mea 'uma, 'auā o lau manava ola le afua ma le 'ato'atoa. O 'oe IOA le fai tagata, le tausi tagata, o oe fo'i 'e pule i le tagata.

O 'oe le fai 'āiga, le fa'atupu 'āiga ma le tasui ma le ulua'i Alii o 'āiga. O oe o le fai nu'u, o oe o le fa'atupu nu'u, o oe fo'i o lē tausi nu'u.

E tapu ma pa'ia oe mai le vavau e o'o i le fa'avavau. O 'oe o le tofi o Sāmoa o matou fo'i o lou tofi mai le lagi. E foi 'iā te 'oe le mālosi, le mana, vi'iga ma le fa'ane'etaga. Amene.

IOA our origin, our root and sovereign supreme Creator in heaven. You alone through your very breath created the immense expanse and the galaxies. By the very sound of your voice the waters, the ocean, the land, the heavens and all things were created. You are the beginning of all things for your very sacred breath was and is the origin and the fullness of all. You are the creator, keeper and sustainer of mankind. You are the origin, who covers, grows and protects our families. You are the very root, multiplier and protector of our tribes and villages. Sacred Sovereign Supreme Creator, the original Alii and Tuitupu (King), you are the beginning and the end. You are from everlasting to everlasting. You are our covenant inheritance and we are yours from heaven. All strength, power and majesty belong to you our Alii and King. Amene.

The above prayer was a regular acknowledgement of the Creator, IOA, passed down from our ancestors and daily practiced every morning at 5am and every evening at 6:30pm by my grandparents and most families in my father's village Sa'asa'ai Āmoa when I was growing up on the island of Savaii in Sāmoa. It is still prayed today daily by our elders in our island nation.

We human beings are incapable of an absolute exact name worthy enough to acknowledge the sacred, holy supreme and sovereign Creator. As Sāmoans and Polynesians the name IOA or IO is the most sacred name our ancestors could offer to Him. Atua (Akua – Hawaiian, God – English) is not the Creator's name. Atua is a general name and a noun given or allocated to any god in the Polynesian triangle such as physical idols or any spiritual being. The god, Tagaloa or Tangaloa, is not the same as IOA as some recent Sāmoans and Polynesians claim. Tagaloa/Tangaloa's story is found in most Polynesians islands. The ancient oral accounts of Tagaloa in Sāmoan history and most Polynesian islands proves that Tagaloa was a powerful but finite being who had many human wives and fought human wars. As a descendant of Tagaloa myself and a holder of the title, Tagaloa, our oral accounts as Sāmoans clearly state that Tagaloa was a powerful, yet finite being who later became a powerful Alli from which our people and my family descended. As the holder of the Alii ancient title, Tagaloa, and a descendent of Tagaloa, I have been redeemed through the transformational mana and power of IOA, the Creator, through His Son, Iēsū Keriso, Jesus Christ. This is a deep subject that will be documented further in a forthcoming book about my people, culture and family.

The Supreme, All-Powerful, Self-Existent, Creator of All gave the finite Hebrew people a name by which to call an Infinite, All Powerful God, *YHWH*. Scholars are still divided about the meaning of that name, some interpret it simply as "I Am," others as "He Brings into Existence Whatever Exists." Both are inadequate to describe the Supreme, All-Powerful, Self-Existent, Creator of All. We, Sāmoans, in our own finiteness, are no different in our human inadequacies to have a name worthy of the Supreme, All-Powerful, Self-Existent, Creator of All. The name given to our Sāmoan ancestors for this

God in our finite linguistic abilities as a people is also inadequate, *IOA*.

Before our many little gods was the great IOA (the Great One). Therefore, when the Bible was translated into Sāmoan (Sāmoan First Edition Bible,1854), IOA was used for the name of the Creator in this first written text book for life and modern education. My ancestors believed that IOA (Exodus 27:16, Sāmoan First Edition Bible) was the name we should use to refer to the Supreme Sovereign Creator who was revealed to us in our cultural story and later personally made known to us through His Son, Iēsū Keriso."

| Some Sāmoan letters and phonetic sounds: | Sāmoan phonetic context: |
|---|---|
| *IOA* | Origin, root and sacred breath/ life, where we came from, where we are and where we are going towards. |
| *i,'i* and *'ī* as in *hi, Sāvai'i, sau 'i 'ī, tu'itu'i, alii* or *Ali'i, 'ia 'ia* and *'iā, atamai, 'aumai,* | *i,'i* and *'ī* speaks of origin and going back to our roots and where we came from as in *Savaii, Savai'i* or *sau i 'i. 'ia* is to agree to what is true and original. *alii, Alii* or *Ali'i* means original blood line or authentic linage. *atamai* or *akamai* is authentic original holistic wisdom or understanding. *'aumai* is to take back to the origin. |

| o, ʻo and ʻō as in mua o, alu ʻi ʻo, ʻō ʻo aʻu lenei, ʻio, iʻo, | o, ʻo, ʻō speaks of divine direction, purpose and hope as in mua o. ʻio speaks of affirming authentic original truth and iʻo or iʻō speaks of root, origin and where something or someone is from. |
|---|---|
| a, ʻa, ʻā as in tālofa, alofa, ʻatofa, sā, vaʻa, ha. | a, ʻa ,ʻā represent sacred breath, declaration, direction or journey as in sā, vaʻa or ʻāāāāā which is the deep original sacred sound. ʻa as in ʻatoa affirms holistic wholeness while a as in tea provokes the sense of transcendent purity, ʻā as in tuaʻā points to where we came from, our ancestors, which is also tupuga. Tālofa is to daily demonstrate and practice the holistic and transcendent spirit of love, wellness, acceptance and forgiveness while a as in atofa is sacred life onwards. |

## Tonga and the Marquesas

I have not spent much time in research on the traditions of 'Io in the Marquesas and Tonga. However, in the Marquesas "io" signifies power. In Tonga, "io" means, "yes, it is true, amen." These may be the surface meanings of deeper kaona as iʻo has in the Cook Islands and in Hawaiʻi .

There seems to be very little of the knowledge of 'Io left in Central Polynesia. Why I say, "seems to be," is because more knowledge may be secreted away within the families of the ancient 'Io priesthood. It seems that Central Polynesia (Tonga, Samoa, Tahiti) was where a later migration of Polynesians brought the cult of Tagaloa. Tagaloa/Tangaloa/Ta'aroa is the Creator God in Central Polynesia although there are still shreds of knowledge of 'Io in Central Polynesia.

# Chapter 7

# Why Are There Different Traditions Of 'Io?

I know of several reasons why there are different traditions of 'Io, there are probably more.

**One**: Recent DNA evidence points to at least three major migrations into Polynesia and possibly four or five smaller ones. Over time, there was the intermingling of 'Io traditions with traditions from other migrations.

For instance, one pre-Pā'ao tradition is very similar to the traditions of the Tamil people of India. They believed they came from a sunken continent, worshipped many gods, their ancestors and believed in reincarnation. Very different than the 'Io traditions and yet there is evidence that these traditions were combined by some.

**Two**: Corruption of the original knowledge of 'Io.

Hawaiian traditions mention the corruption of the 'Io religion before Pā'ao arrived in the tradition of 'Aikanaka,

Hema and Kaha'i, three famous navigators and priests of 'Io. Hema had a twin brother, *Puna*. Ahu'ena Taylor, a descendant of the priesthood of 'Io, claims Hema as an ancestor. It was passed down to her that "*'Io left Hawai'i when the chieftain Hema departed for New Zealand to live after his feudal warfare with his brother Puna.*" She also said, "*Hema did not worship as his gods the guardians of the sea, fresh water, or mountains; so 'Io loved him and went away with him.*"[43] This may also be why there is so much more 'Io knowledge in New Zealand than in Hawai'i. It seems the corruption of pure 'Io worship was on its way before Pā'ao arrived.

A kupuna of the family whose ancient burial grounds are at South Point (*Ka Lae*) on the Big Island, one of the oldest burial sites in Hawai'i, told me that there used to be two standing stones outside of the burial grounds. These stones were named *Kū* and *Hina* because they represented, *Kū*, the strength and, *Hina*, the wisdom of their God to bring them to Hawai'i. Later, *Kū* and *Hina* became a pair of gods instead of aspects of the One God.

It seems that the worship of 'Io alone, his chants and traditions were later combined with the worship of Kū and other gods during the time of the Kapu System. Sometimes Kū and 'Io were worshipped together and/or 'Io's titles and chants were altered into Kū chants.

Handy writes that "*According to Ahu'ena (and likewise Pu'uheana) the name of 'Io or Iolani was purposely camouflaged by means of pseudonyms. 'Io was referred to as Ili-o-mea-lani (the reflection of that chiefly someone), Kū'e-manu-ai-lehua (the beak that feeds on lehuas or the power of death), and Uli (eternity, chaos, beyond vision). With respect to Ili-o-mea-lani, Ahu'ena made the following*

*observations in discussing the prayers with me in 1932.*
*The epithet may be translated Reflection-of-someone-of-*
*Heaven, ili having the sense of aka (shadow, similitude).*
*Others have maintained, incorrectly according to Ahu'ena,*
*that the spelling should be Ilio-mea-lani. Paahana, on her*
*own independent authority, states that Ili-o-mea-lani is*
*'Io, whereas Ilio-mea-lani is the dog (ilio) embodiment of*
*the god Kū.*"[44]

One might say, "*How can this happen when man was*
*sacred to 'Io and not to be killed? How can 'Io worship*
*and Kū worship be combined when Kū was a god that*
*demanded human sacrifice?*"

Let's look at an example from another people, the people
of Israel. God, Yahweh, told Noah when he came out of the
ark, "*You will not kill man because he is made in my image.*"
Yet, during times of corruption in Israel, Yahweh worship
was corrupted to the point that the Hebrews worshipped
Yahweh, Baal, Tammuz, Ashtoreth and Molech (2 Kings
17:16-17, 1 Kings 11:5-7, Ezekiel 8:14) and other gods in
the very temple of Yahweh (2 Kings 23:4). Humans were
sacrificed to Baal, Tammuz, Ashtoreth and Molech. Should
the God, Yahweh, be thrown out of the Bible because of
this? Should Yahweh be thrown out because at Mizpah, the
temples of Asherah and Yahweh were erected side by side?
Or because, in the Jewish Elephantine community in Egypt,
the Canaanite goddesses, *Anat-Yahu* (or *Anat-Bethel*),
*Ashim-Bethel* and *Haram-Bethel* were assigned to Yahweh
as consorts and the lesser gods procreated through these
unions?[45] Or, should Jews and Christians instead preserve
and restore this precious name of God to its original purity?

Therefore, somehow, this form of corruption can happen. In some 'Io traditions, 'Io has children. How can this

be if he is *'Io-lala-'ole* ('Io without branches/children)? Stimson wrote that in the oldest Kiho traditions of the Tuamotus and the oldest 'Io traditions of the Maori, 'Io had no parents, no wife, no offspring.[46]

**Three**: Turning "*Akua,*" into gods.

Fornander stated about the word "*Akua,*" "*...Akua did not convey the same lofty idea as the word God or Deity does to the Christian. To the Hawaiians the word Akua expressed the idea of any supernatural being...*"[47]

In the book, "*Tohunga: Hohepa Kereopa,*" Hohepa explains, "*...in Maori, anyone who does good to you is an atua* (akua in Hawaiian dialect) – *it has a different meaning from English...*"[48] Hohepa dedicated himself entirely to the will of the Almighty (God). He also believed that Jesus Christ is God's Son who God sacrificed so his people would come back to him.[49]

*Timoti Robinson* states in the book, *Tohunga,* when prayers to 'Io went unanswered, "*they* (Maori) *turned to lesser atua to gain favors. 'Io does not favor every person but only a few who are just...it was men that deified these atua into gods* (Emphasis, the author's)."[50] This statement parallels Fornander's statement about the word *akua*. Te Whatahoro stated, "*We have seen that no form of image or representation of Io was ever made by the Maori, such an act was inadmissible. Nor did he have any form of aria, that is any visible form, or form of incarnation* (Kino Lau), *such as the lower gods, ancestral spirits, had. Images pertained to the departmental gods. Nor were there any sacrifices or offerings made to Io, though they were to lower gods.*"[51]

According to Robinson, there was initially only one God, 'Io. Then men deified other atua (spiritual beings) into gods. Hence, 'Io being worshipped at the same time as other "gods." In the Bible, when men saw an angel in their glorious state, they fell like dead men before them. Mat. 28:2-4 NKJV says," *And behold, there was a great earthquake, for an angel of the Lord descended from heaven and came and rolled back the stone from the door, and sat on it. His countenance was like lightning, and his clothing white as snow. And the guards shook for fear of him and became like dead men.*" It would not be difficult to see how men could deify the servants of 'Io or "fallen" servants of 'Io.

Norman and To'o record, "*Io had nothing to do with anything evil. All evil emanated from the minor atua.*" Best comments that "*In the beginning all men invoked Io and sought his aid, but when they found that many of their prayers were not granted, they invoked minor gods and demons, and sought their aid. Such were the teach-*

Te Matorohanga

*ings of Te Matorohanga, the last first class Tohunga of the East Coast. Such is the Maori explanation of polytheism, of a people originally monotheistic evolving a polytheistic cult.*"[52]

Akua/Atua not being equivalent to the Western concept of God is not unusual. For instance, the Japanese
word used for God is Kami. However, Kami just means
something or someone with mana (Spiritual power). This
is why the Emperor is a Kami and Mount Fuji is a Kami,
but they are not the Western interpretation of "gods."

A well-known and respected Hawaiian cultural practitioner, whose name I am not at liberty to reveal, was at a
celebration of Hawaiian cultural arts. Some people were
talking about 'Io and he said, *"'Io is not an akua."* My
friend asked him, *"Then who is 'Io."* He replied, *"He just,
is."* This is very similar to the answer Moses received when
he asked the God of the Bible what his name was, *"I Am."*

**Four**: Turning ancestors and forces of nature into gods

Like many people groups around the world, Polynesians
eventually deified ancestor heroes like *Papa* and *Wākea*,
and *Maui* who are in the genealogies of the Polynesians.

Papa and Wākea in other traditions are the Earth
Mother (Papa) and Sky Father (Wākea, *Rangi* in the Maori
– both meaning Heaven). Best states about the Maori Papa
and Rangi, *"There are, for example, two widely differing
versions of cosmogonic and anthrogenic myths pertaining
to the origin of the universe and of man. In the one case
the universe was brought into being by means of the direct
agency of the great demiurge, Io the Supreme Being. In the
other, the primal parents, Rangi and Papa, were the result
of an evolutionary process, which was explained in the
form of a cosmogonic genealogy. Now it was always the
superior version of a myth that was taught by the higher
school of learning [whare wananga]. That school was a
remarkably conservative institution, and the high class*

*cult of Io was confined to the superior order of priestly experts and to superior families. This fact explains how it was that the aforesaid cult of Io was saved from deterioration. Inferior or puerile versions of myths were acquired by the ordinary people; superior versions were retained by the few."*[53]

Therefore, instead of just respecting awesome forces of nature, many Hawaiians, Maori and other native people began to worship them as gods. Several kūpuna told me that these forces of nature were given names so the common people could relate to them, these later became worshipped as gods.

There is confusion also because the names for some of these forces of nature were also the names of famous ancestors like Papa, Wākea and Pele.

# Chapter 8

# Pāʻao And The Kapu System

## Pāʻao

Although every society has its problems, and it seems that the worship of ʻIo was already corrupting, the evidence shows that the Hawaiians remembered the One Supreme God and worshiped him in relative peace until the priest *Pāʻao* came. Fornander writes of this pre-Pāʻao period that *"...the kapus were few and the ceremonials easy; that human sacrifices were not practised, and cannibalism unknown; and that government was more of a patriarchal than of a regal nature."*[54]

The historian, *Rudy Mitchell* (a descendant of Pāʻao), wrote that Pāʻao was a *"High Priest, High Ariʻi (Aliʻi), navigator and sorcerer."* He was an aliʻi nui of the sacred and powerful royal family of *Raʻiatea. Raʻiatea* is an island in the Society Group of islands. This group of islands is more commonly known by the main island of that group, *Tahiti.*

91

The ancient name of *Ra'iatea* was *Havai'i* (This has also caused confusion about Polynesian history). Pā'ao was from *Vavau* (Bora Bora). In ancient times, the royal clan of Vavau conquered the other islands of Western Tahiti and established themselves at Ra'iatea. Although this family knew of 'Io[55], they established a new oppressive religious system with its chief place at *Taputapuatea*.

Most historians estimate that Pā'ao came from *Havai'i* around A.D. 1100 - 1300. He arrived with his warriors, kāhunas and new ali'i. It seems that the earlier voyagers from Tahiti integrated more peacefully with early Hawaiians. Apparently, there was intermarriage with the existing inhabitants and the diminishing of class distinction between the Tahitian ali'i and the earlier migrations.

The traditions say that when Pā'ao arrived, he saw islands ripe for conquer. The people were peaceful. There was no powerful royal house or warriors trained for conquest. He returned to Ra'iatea to bring a new line of ali'i with untainted mana.[56] Malia Craver (a descendant of Pā'ao and also of earlier Hawaiians) was told by her elders that Pā'ao brought many warriors with him.

To consolidate his power, Pā'ao instituted human sacrifices and changed the Hawaiians' religious rituals. He built the first *luakini* (human sacrifice) *heiau* on the Big Island (Hawai'i) at *Waha'ula*.[57] Fornander wrote that "... *there was a time before that, when human sacrifices were not only not of common occurrence, and an established rule, but were absolutely prohibited...*"[58]

# The Kapu System

When Pā'ao conquered Hawai'i, he gave the priests of 'Io three choices:

**One: Resist and die** (The Hawaiian historian Kepelino wrote that "*all the priests of the old religion were killed*").

**Two: Join him and keep your priestly rank**. However, now you must worship his gods and do human sacrifices on the sacred heiau to 'Io, to whom man was sacred and not to be killed. (I have found several families of the priests of 'Io that took this choice).

**Three: Step down** from your priestly rank, become a lowly maka'āinana and never speak of 'Io again (This last group passed the knowledge of 'Io in secret to one child in each generation, the *Pono One*, on pain of death).

Pā'ao instituted the oppressive Kapu System and the worship of elemental spirit gods such as *Pele*. Fornander says that Pele worship in Hawai'i is only subsequent to this migratory period. Pele was also the name of an ancestor who came with this migration. The Pele cult was unknown to the purer faith of the older inhabitants and her name does not appear in the creation accounts.

The class separation between the ali'i and the maka'āinana became a huge gulf. Whereas, under the religion of 'Io, the ali'i were like parents unto the common people.

Fornander wrote, "*In the polity of government initiated during this period, and strengthened as ages rolled on, may be noted the hardening and confirming the divisions of society, the exaltation of the nobles and the increase of their prerogatives, the separation and immunity of the priestly order, and the systematic setting down, if not actual debasement, of the commoners, the maka'āinana.*"[59]

What most people today regard as the religious system of the Hawaiian people, was not their true religion — it was a foreign religion introduced by Pā'ao. Pā'ao's voyages from Tahiti were the last from other Polynesian islands.

Death of a Kapu Breaker

The ali'i convinced the maka'āinana that they had inherited divine power and were divinely chosen by the gods to rule. The Kapu System was structured around the concept of protecting the *mana*. Complex kapu had to be kept to preserve mana. Although ali'i usually kept the kapu, they did this because the belief in mana and the kapu was what kept them in power. High ali'i were never put to death for breaking kapu, although maka'āinana were sometimes sacrificed to correct the "*imbalance in the mana*" caused by an ali'i's sin.

Kapu dictated that men and women had to eat separately and were each restricted to only certain foods. As mentioned earlier, maka'āinana women faced death for eating bananas, coconuts and other foods. Maka'āinana men also faced death for eating certain fish and other foods. If a maka'āinana stepped on ali'i land (even if the boundary was not marked), or if an ali'i shadow fell on him (or his on an ali'i), he was also put to death.[60] Even little children who did not know any better were put to death without grace or mercy.

Death of a Kapu Breaker

An ali'i could take maka'āinana who committed any of these "sins" and use them for human sacrifice or even bait for shark hunting.[61] There were imu (earth ovens) for burning humans at *Punchbowl* and *Waikiki*.[62] Maka'āinana were drowned at *Kewalo Basin* (Honolulu) for breaking kapu.[63] Human heads, of those offered in sacrifice, were put on stakes that lined the *Pakaka* heiau at the foot of Fort Street (Downtown Honolulu) as they did on most Luakini heiau.[64] At the heiau located at the foot of Diamond Head, men had their limbs broken with clubs, their eyes scooped out, and then were left bleeding and maimed for three days. They were later clubbed to death with blows to the shoulders rather than to the head, thus prolonging their suffering before death.[65]

The executioners of the Kapu System, the *Mū*, filled the maka'āinana with terror. When human sacrifices were needed, they would sneak around the villages looking for anyone who broke a kapu or was speaking negatively about the ali'i or kāhuna. If this was not successful, they would try to entice a maka'āinana to come out of his hut with lies. If the person came out, the Mū would put a hook in his mouth and drag this *"long legged fish"* to the heiau for sacrifice.[66]

The maka'āinana had no rights and nothing they could call their own. An ali'i could take anything he wanted from a maka'āinana: his food, his belongings, his favorite pig, his children—or even his wife. The ali'i could "tax" most of a maka'āinana's food away and force him to work on his building projects. It is estimated that two-thirds of what the maka'āinana produced was taken by high ali'i, chiefs and kāhunas. The maka'āinana were so maltreated that when some of the first anthropologists arrived, they thought that the Hawaiians were comprised of two different races - the huge ali'i and the scrawny maka'āinana.[67]

Not only were these harsh requirements put on the maka'āinana, but they were constantly drafted into armies to fight when the ali'i wanted more power. Under the previous religion of 'Io, society was peaceful. Captured maka'āinana were used as slaves or for sacrifice. The Hawaiian people were also decimated by these wars. By the time of Kamehameha, there had been some 300 years of nearly constant warfare.[68]

John Young, Kamehameha's trusted foreign advisor, said in 1826 of the conditions he had observed during his forty-nine years in Hawai'i, "*I have known thousands of defenseless human beings cruelly massacred in their exterminating wars. I have seen multitudes...offered in sacrifice to their idol gods...*"[69]

While man was sacred to 'Io and not to be killed. Pā'ao instituted human sacrifice, mostly to *Kū*. It seems that at some unknown time after Pā'ao arrived, Kū was changed into a vengeful and bloodthirsty god of war.[70] Both Fornander and Pukui state that before Pā'ao's arrival, Kū was benign.

As mentioned in the previous chapter, a kupuna whose ancient burial grounds are at South Point (*Ka Lae*) on the Big Island told me that there used to be two standing stones outside of the burial grounds. These stones were named *Kū* and *Hina* because they represented, *Kū*, the strength and, *Hina*, the wisdom of their God to bring them to Hawai'i. Later, *Kū* and *Hina* became a pair of separate gods instead of aspects of the One God.

*Chapter 9*

# The True God of Hawai'i Comes in His New Form

## Prophecies

Six Hawaiian *Kāula* (Prophets) had given 12 prophecies concerning the new God prior to the overthrow of the Kapu System and before the coming of the missionaries who would bring this prophesied God.

The Hawaiian scholar, John Henry Wise, recounted an ancient prophecy for an article in the Honolulu Star Bulletin in 1923, "...*And the time will come when the people will forsake their true God; but he will not forsake his people. He will return to them in the form of a square box, and the people will not know that within the box dwells their God* (prophecy #1)." The article continues, "*Thus runs an ancient saying of the Hawaiians – a saying so old that it is believed to antedate the remote period in which began the gradual disintegration of the original island religion...*" It seems that this prophecy antedated the arrival of Pā'ao and the Kapu System.[71]

Another Kāula prophesied the Hawaiian God of Peace (*Lono*) would return in a new form. He would return in a small black box and speak a language that they would not understand (prophecy #2).[72] There is evidence that this prophecy was given by *Hewahewa*, the last *Kahuna Nui*, high priest, of the Kapu System.

*Kahu Matt Higa*, a descendant of *Hewahewa*, was told about the *Black Box Prophecy* by *Koko Willis*, Caretaker at the Bishop Museum, who cared for ancient Hawaiian artifacts. Matt is related to Koko Willis through his brother's wife. Koko told him when he was still in high school (1975-78) about this prophecy with different details than others recorded. Koko Willis, upon learning from Matt's genealogy that he was a descendant of Hewahewa, shared with him the following information about Hewahewa. Koko told Matt that Hewahewa had a vision. He told Kamehameha that "*A God greater than his would come on a canoe bigger than his* (prophecy #3.)," and that "*this God would come in a box* (possibly repeating the ancient prophecy)."

Koko Willis was one of the few people who knew where Hewahewa's body was buried in Waimea Valley on O'ahu. He obviously had privy information about Hewahewa that most did not know. Matt also did not ask Koko about the Black Box; this information was offered by Koko.

In her introduction to the Kumulipo genealogy chant, Queen Lili'uokalani says that a prophecy was sung by Puou, Kahuna Nui and father of Hewahewa, to Captain Cook. Lili'uokalani writes, "*For it was prophesied by priests at the time of the death of Ka-I-i-mamao* (Mid-1700s, before the time of Hewahewa.) *that he, Lono, would return anew from the sea in a Spanish man-of-war or Auwaalalua* (prophecy

#4). *To the great navigator they accordingly gave a welcome with the name of Lono.*" Ka-I-i-mamao was Ali'i Nui of the district of Ka'ū where many of the descendants of the priesthood of 'Io come from. Lili'uokalani continues, "*The chanters of this great poem were Hewahewa and Ahukai.*"[73] The prophecy that Lono would return in a box seems to have been connected to the return of Lono after Captain Cook's arrival or the Hawaiians would have known that Cook did not fulfill the return of Lono. The prophecy of Lono's return may have been connected with the prophecy of the true God returning in a square box by Hewahewa after Cook's death.

The kahuna *Maliu* prophesied when he forgot his idol after a heiau service, "*An overthrow will be the result of this neglect of the deity, an event the like of which was never seen before* (prophecy #5)." Upon hearing of Maliu's prophetic utterance, Hewahewa also prophesied, "*There will be an overthrow in the future; no greater reverses will ever occur than the one forthcoming* (prophecy #6)."[74]

A generation before the overthrow, another Kāula, *Kalaikuahulu*, said that a communication would be made from heaven by *Ke Akua Maoli*, the True God.[75] This communication would be entirely different than anything they had ever known (prophecy #7). He also prophesied the overthrow of the Kapu System (prophecy #8).

Another Kāula, *Kapihe*, announced in Kamehameha's presence about three years before he unified Hawai'i that "*The ancient kapu will be overthrown, the heiau and lele altars will be overthrown, and the images will fall down. God will be in the heavens; the Islands will unite, the chiefs will fall, and those of the earth (the lesser people) will rise* (prophecy #9)." [76]

## The Overthrow of the Kapu System

Kamehameha unified the islands as prophesied, but he maintained the Kapu System of Pāʻao. Why did he do this when Kamehameha also knew of ʻIo? When asked by Chief *Kuakini* why he didn't change the harsh religious practices, especially of human sacrifice, Kamehameha replied, *"You don't think me such a fool as to put any faith in their efficacy. I only suffer them because I find them useful in keeping my people in subjection."*[77]

According to King *Kalākaua*, in the latter part of the reign of Kamehameha I, the gods and the kapu of the priesthood began to lose respect. Although no clear idea of Christianity had been imparted to the Hawaiians by the sailors and traders, the foreigner's disregard of the kapu was observed to bring no punishment. The Hawaiians began to question their gods and religion.

Kalākaua continues, *"The results of this growing scepticism were frequent violations of the tabu. To check this seditious tendency summary punishments were inflicted. A woman was put to death for entering the eating apartment of her husband, and Jarvis relates that three men were sacrificed at Kealakeakua, a short time before the death of Kamehameha—one of them for putting on the maro of a chief, another for eating a forbidden article, and the third for leaving a house that was tabu and entering one that was not."* When Kamehameha was questioned about Christianity during his last illness, he replied that *"he should die in the faith of his fathers, although he thought it well that his successor should give the subject attention."*[78]

Kamehameha set in motion the overthrow of the Kapu System by forbidding death companions for himself when he died. By rejecting this practice of killing wives, friends and servants so they could accompany a High Chief into the afterlife, he was defying the old system. It seems that Kamehameha and Hewahewa, who both knew of 'Io, were *"caught"* in the religious system of their ancestors that had been in place for some 600 years. Changing an entire religious system, system of government and culture into something unknown to them would be difficult even though some of the highest ali'i in the land were ready and desiring this change.

Liholiho

After Kamehameha died, his son, *Liholiho* became King. Liholiho knew of the growing hostility to the Kapu System. He had talked with Hewahewa on the subject. He learned that his mother had lately failed to keep the kapu in private and had himself seen it violated without harm to the offender. Kalākaua continues, *"Yet he feared the consequences of an open declaration against the priesthood. He remembered the fate of Hua, whose bones whitened in the sun."*[79] When the King fears to change the entrenched religious system, it is clear how difficult this change would be.

However, after Kamehameha died, two of his wives, *Ke'ōpūolani* and *Ka'ahumanu*, and the new King Liholiho broke the kapu as prophesied. At the feast when the kapu was openly broken, *"Hewahewa rose, and, glancing at the troubled face of the king, lifted his hands and said with firmness: 'One and all, may we eat in peace, and in our hearts give thanks to the one and only god of all.'*[80]

Kalākaua continues, "*At the conclusion of the royal feast a still greater surprise bewildered the people. 'We have made a bold beginning,' said Hewahewa to the king, thus adroitly assuming a part of the responsibility; 'but the gods and heiaus cannot survive the death of the tabu.' 'Then let them perish with it!' exclaimed Liholiho, now nerved to desperation at what he had done. 'If the gods can punish, we have done too much already to hope for grace. They can but kill, and we will test their powers by inviting the full measure of their wrath. To this resolution the high-priest gave his ready assent, and orders were issued at once for the destruction of the gods and temples throughout the kingdom. Resigning his office, Hewahewa was the first to apply the torch, and in the smoke of burning heiaus, images and other sacred property, beginning on Hawaii and ending at Niihau,*"[81]

Kamehameha's most sacred wife, Ke'ōpūolani said, "*Our gods have done us no good; they are cruel.*"[82] Hewahewa said, "*I knew the wooden images of deities, carved by our own hands, could not supply our wants, but worshipped them because it was a custom of our fathers... My thought has always been, there is one only great God, dwelling in the heavens.*"[83]

James Hunnewell Jr., wrote an account of this incident that he received directly from his father who was the First Mate on the Thaddeus (the ship that brought the missionaries). His father had personal conversations with Hewahewa. The following account of what happened was told to James Hunnewell Jr. by his father who was given this account by Hewahewa "*...before the missionaries landed...This chief of the old idolatrous system said that he* *knew that the wooden gods could not send rain, or cause food to grow, or send fish, or take care of the old men and women; and he added that he knew that there was but one great God dwelling in the heavens. ('Akahi wale nō Akua-nui iloko o ka lani.") Having this belief and practicing the old system, because, as he said, it was an observance of Hawaiians, he conversed on the subject with the King Kamehameha II, and after very guarded approaches to avowals* (confirmation), *each ascertained that their belief was the same."* [84]

These statements of Kamehameha, Hewahewa and Ke'ōpūolani, whose descendants confirm that they knew of 'Io, confirms to us that the kāhuna and ali'i knew the ways of the gods of the Kapu System were wrong. This is further confirmed by the following story.

When Chiefess *Kapi'olani* was a young girl she ate a banana, breaking a kapu because women were not allowed to eat bananas. But because she was a high ali'i, Kapi'olani was not put to death. Instead, a kahuna took her favorite servant, a child named Mau, and strangled him on the altar of the heiau. Many years later, after the over-throw of the Kapu System, Kapi'olani was one of the first to accept Iesū Kristo (Jesus Christ). After becoming a follower of Jesus, she asked the kahuna who had strangled her friend Mau why he had done this. The kahuna replied, *"Those were dark days, **though we priests knew better all the time** (emphasis, the author's)."* The kahuna continued, ***"It was power we sought over the minds of the people, to influence and control them** (emphasis, the author's)."* Kapi'olani hid her face in her hands and wept.[85]

The new king, Liholiho; Kamehameha's sacred wife, Ke'ōpūolani; his favorite wife, Ka'ahumanu; together with

Hewahewa, the Kahuna Nui; and *Kalanimoku*, the Prime
Minister, initiated sweeping changes. The Kapu System
was abolished, the heiaus were destroyed, and human sacrifice and death for breaking kapu was ended.

Hawai'i was suspended in a spiritual void. Sometime
during this period, Hewahewa pronounced the tenth prophecy. While walking on the shore of *Kailua* Bay (anciently
known as *Kai-a-Ke-Akua*, The Sea of God) with the new
King Liholiho, Hewahewa pointed to a rock and said,
*"Here O King, the New God shall come* (prophecy #10)."
After announcing that the new god was coming, he left to
await the arrival of a *"new and greater god"* at his home in
*Kawaiahae* (prophecy #11). [86]

# Chapter 10

# The New God Arrives

Just 20 days after the breaking of the kapu, the first missionary company, made up of Hawaiians and *Haole* (foreigners), embarked for Hawai'i. This mission was launched because of a young Hawaiian man, *'Ōpūkaha'ia*, who, although he died in New England, so inspired the missionaries that they left everything they knew to fulfill his dream. 'Ōpūkaha'ia had personally experienced the terrors of the Kapu System and was able to escape to New

OBOOKIAH,

A NATIVE OF OWHYHEE.

England on an American ship. He learned about the God of the Bible there. His ardent desire and dream was for his people to know this God. Instead of gods who demanded the blood of Hawaiians in sacrifice to them, this God shed his blood and laid down His life for Hawaiians.[87]

When the missionaries' ship was off shore at Kawaiahae, Hewahewa exclaimed, "*The New God is coming*" (prophecy #12) and left Kawaiahae to meet them at Kailua Bay.[88]

Of this account, J.S. Emerson gives this version in his *Selections from a Kahuna's Book of Prayer*, Hawaiian Historical Society, 1917. "*A few days before the missionaries landed at Kailua he (Hewahewa) foresaw their coming and instructed his awa chewer to run in front of the house, near the shore where the royal family were living, and call out, 'E ka lani e, ina aku ke akua a pae mai.' O King, the god will soon land yonder, pointing, as he spoke, to the very spot on the sandy beach* (It is not clear if this was a separate incident from the previously recorded one, prophecy #13?) *where, a few days later, April 4th, 1820, the little band of missionaries landed from the brig Thaddeus, bringing with them the new god. In commemoration of this incident the spot received the name, 'Kai-o-ke-akua* (The older name of Kailua Bay),' *the sea of the god, by which name it has ever since been called. During the next few days the missionaries had audience with royalty and earnestly presented the claims of their god for the worship of the people. Their pleading made such an impression on the high chiefess, Kapi'olani nui, that she told Hewahewa that the god had really landed, and expressed her willingness to accept the new religion. This led Hewahewa, the chief religious leader of the kingdom, to prepare this prayer as a welcome to the new god who had so recently arrived."*

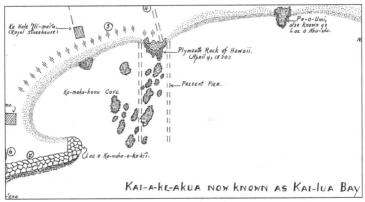

Map by Henry E.P. Kehahuna

## A PRAYER ANTE-DATING THE USE OF THE LORD'S PRAYER IN HAWAI'I.

*"Arise, stand up, stand.*
*Fill up the ranks, stand in rows, stand.*
*Lest we be in darkness, in black night.*
*Ye thorny-hearted, assemble, a multitude, stand.*
*A great God, a mighty God,*
*A living God, an everlasting God,*
*Is Jehovah, a Visitor from the skies;*
*A God dwelling afar off, in the heights,*
*At the further end of the wind,*
*In the rolling cloud, floating in air.*
*A light cloud resting on the earth,*
*A rainbow standing in the ocean,*
*Is Jesus, Our Redeemer.*
*By the path from Kahiki (a foreign land) to us in*
*Hawaii He comes.*

*From the zenith to the horizon;*
*A mighty rain from the heavens,*
*Jehovah the Supreme, we welcome.* **(Knowing that Hewahewa knew of 'Io, I believe this translation should be** *"Jehovah, 'I , our desire fulfilled."***)**
*Sing praises to the rolling heavens.*
*Now the earth rejoices.*
*We have received the words*
*Of knowledge, of power, of life.*
*Gather in the presence of Poki,*
*In the presence of the ever mighty Lord.*
*Pray with reverence to Jehovah,*
*As a mighty kahuna of the Islands,*
*Who, like a torch, shall reveal our great sins;*
*That we all may live;*
*Live through Jesus.*
*Amen.*

The Missionary *Elisha Loomis* wrote of Hewahewa, *"Who could have expected that such would have been our first interview with the man whose influence we had been accustomed to dread more than any other in the islands; whom we had regarded and could now hardly help regarding as a deceiver of his fellow men. But he seemed much pleased in speaking of the destruction of the heiau and idols."* *"About five months ago the young king consulted him with respect to the expediency of breaking taboo and asked him to tell him frankly and plainly whether it would be good or bad, assuring him at the same time that he would be guided by his view."* *"Hewahewa speedily replied, maikai it would be good, adding that he knew there is but one "Akoohah"* (Akua) *who is in heaven, and that their wooden gods could not save them nor do them any good." "He publicly renounced idolatry and with his own hand set fire to the heiau. The king no more observed their superstitious taboos."*[89]

The rock Hewahewa prophesied the missionaries would land on still remains under the current Kailua pier (See the drawing above). It has been dubbed, the Plymouth Rock of Hawai'i. The first missionary to step out onto the rock was Hiram Bingham. He was carrying a black Bible box in front of him. Bibles were hand pressed at this time and so were family heirlooms. They were kept in protective boxes especially on long sea voyages. Again, it seems that it was

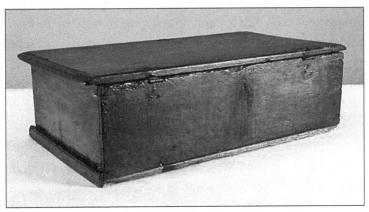

Bible Box

Hewahewa who prophesied the Hawaiian God of Peace (*Lono*) would return in a new form. He would return in a small black box and speak a language that they would not understand.[90] When the box was opened, Hewahewa and the kāhuna could not understand what was written there and proclaimed that the prophecy was fulfilled. Lono, the god of Peace, the Hawaiians True/First God, had returned in his new form. It must be stressed that it was not the imperfect missionaries who fulfilled this prophecy, it was the God spoken of in the book they brought, the Bible.

It is an amazing fact that it was the descendants of Pā'ao and Pili (the ali'i line of chiefs that came with Pā'ao), who were the very ones with the courage and prophetic foresight to break the Hawaiian people free from the entrenched and feared religious system of their ancestors. They were the first to accept the new God, Iesū Kristo; Ke Akua Maoli, the True God of the Hawaiians (as prophesied by *Kalaikuahulu*), had come in his new form that was different from anything they had known before.

If the highest Hawaiian ali'i did not foresee this change and in unity break the kapu, it is doubtful that the missionaries would have been given permission to remain in Hawai'i. If the missionaries were not inspired to come by 'Ōpūkaha'ia, it is doubtful they would have come to Hawai'i. If Hawaiians were not a part of that first company of missionaries to communicate to the ali'i and teach Hawaiian to the missionaries, it is in doubt that the missionaries would have been allowed to remain. If the high Christian Tahitian chief, Taua, and Christian Tahitian teachers did not come to Hawai'i from the land of Pā'ao and Pili to share the gospel in a language the Hawaiians could understand, Iesū may not have been accepted. If Taua did not affirm that the new religion has been good in Tahiti, Iesū may have not been accepted. If Taua had not discipled Ke'ōpūolani, the highest ali'i in the land, Iesū may not have been accepted. If Ke'ōpūolani was not the first to be baptized and did not instruct her sons, the king and future king, to protect the missionaries and love Iesū, Iesū may not have been accepted in Hawai'i. Not enough credit is given to the chiefly descendants of Pāʻao and Pili, ʻŌpūkahaʻia, the Hawaiians who were in the first company of missionaries and the Tahitian Christian teachers for the acceptance of Iesū Kristo in Hawaiʻi.

# Chapter 11

# God of Light, God of Darkness

As previously mentioned, when Pāʻao conquered Hawaiʻi, he gave the priests of ʻIo three choices:

**Resist and die** (The Hawaiian historian Kepelino wrote that "*all the priests of the old religion were killed*")

**Join him and keep your priestly rank.** However, now you must worship his gods and do human sacrifices on the sacred heiau to ʻIo to whom man was sacred and not to be killed. (I have found several families of the priests of ʻIo that took this choice).

**Step down** from your priestly rank, become a lowly makaʻāinana (commoner) and never speak of ʻIo again (This last group passed the knowledge of ʻIo in secret to one child in each generation, the Pono One, on pain of death).

The legacy of a family of the priesthood of 'Io who took this third choice is recorded in the book, *God of Light, God of Darkness*. The *Iokane* (A Pseudonym) family held an 800-year-old prophecy of 'Io. When Pā'ao arrived and gave the priests of 'Io the three choices, the Kahuna Nui of their family prayed to 'Io asking what he should do. His answer was a prophecy, "*Step down for someday, a descendant of yours will restore this heiau to the worship of me.*" This prophecy was fulfilled in 1998 by a Christian descendant of that Kahuna Nui who was the "*Pono One*" of his family. The prophecy was fulfilled with the Biblical ritual of Communion and accompanied by many miracles, signs and wonders.

The fulfilling of the prophecy was witnessed by 150 people. It is the strongest primary source evidence that the God 'Io is the same God as the God of the Bible. The imperfect and very human missionaries were simply the vehicle which brought the return of 'Io to the Hawaiian people in his new form, Iesū Kristo, Jesus Christ.

# Chapter 12

# Is 'Io the same Creator God of the Bible?

Having my Ph.D. in Intercultural Studies from seminary, I have studied many native people from around the world and their traditions in relationship to the Bible. I think Romans 1:20 should be repeated here, *"For since the creation of the world God's invisible qualities, his eternal power and divine nature, have been clearly seen, being understood from what has been made, so that people are without excuse."* It would be unbiblical if the Polynesians did not have knowledge of the One Creator God of all.

Twelve Hawaiian prophecies were fulfilled in the coming of the God of the Bible. There were also prophecies about the coming of a new religion that would change everything in Samoa and Tahiti. There was also a prophecy in New Zealand which will be presented in a later chapter. I am sure there are more but these are all I have found in my limited research in Polynesia. Besides these, there are other evidences. There are many Hawaiian,

Genesis-like, traditions that were recorded by the oldest and best sources; Fornander, Kalākaua, Kepilino, Malo and Kamakau. However, because these traditions were so much like the Bible stories and 'Io so much like the God of the Bible, they have been rejected and "buried" by secular humanist researchers. To read about the many Genesis-like traditions from native people around the world and in Hawai'i, read *Perpetuated In Righteousness*.

The Bible says that all people could clearly see God's invisible qualities, his eternal power and divine nature. In every people group that I have been able to spend the time to research, I have found this to be true. The problem is that most missionaries and Christians do not take the time to research these. Job, who was a native man, not a Jew, and did not have the Jewish scriptures, said *"For I know that my Redeemer lives, and that in the end he will stand on the earth."* (Job 19:25 NIV). Many people groups knew that the Creator had a Son including the Hawaiians (This will be explained in the section on King Kauikeaouli) and Maori. Although, the full mystery of Jesus and what he would do was not known to them (Col. 1:26-27). Maori Historian *Charlie Matthews*, shared with me an ancient Maori chant that said, *"'Io Matua, 'Io Tama Akaaka"* - *'Io the Father, 'Io the Son the Vine*. This was not a sexually procreated son like the other gods of Polynesia had, but this Son was 'Io himself. Jesus is also called The Vine in the Bible (John 15:1-8).

In 1766, three years before Captain Cook arrived in Aotearoa, a Maori prophet named Toiroa declared a strange people will bring a new God. *"The name of their God will be Tama-i-rorokutia (Son-who-was-killed), a good God, however the people will still be oppressed.*[91]

Some people even knew that the Creator's Son would do something wonderful for them. They had what is known in missiology as the "General Revelation" of God but not the "Specific Revelation" that comes from the Bible. The full mystery of what this Son would do was not known to them. In my research, I have found that many people around the world including different Native American tribes, different African tribes, Koreans and many Muslim people have had dreams and visions of Jesus as they were seeking to know their Creator more. My mentor, Don Richardson, wrote in his book *Eternity in Their Hearts* a tradition of the Mbaka people of the Central African Republic, *"Koro, the Creator, sent word to our forefathers long ages ago that He has already sent His Son into the world to accomplish something wonderful for all mankind."* The Bible says in two places (Rev. 13:8, 1Peter 1:19-21) that Jesus, was the lamb slain from the foundation of the world.

One of the names of 'Io recorded by Fornander in Hawai'i was *Uli*, meaning *Eternity, Beyond.*[92]* In one of the prayers Emerson recorded, Uli is correlated with Iku, *"Uli, the active, the multiform, offshoot of Iku, Iku, king of kings in heaven, broken for others..."* Emerson writes that *Iku* means *the highest, the head of all."* [93] Therefore, possibly, 'I-ku, The Supreme Ruler. Jesus is the *"Lamb slain from the foundation of the world."*

In *Nā Inoa Hōkū, A Catalogue of Hawaiian and Pacific Star Names*, the North Star is called in Hawaiian, *Hōkū Pa'a* (The Star That Does Not Move). The North Star is the only star in the sky that does not move. All the other stars of the heavens revolve around it. It is the center of the heavens. Two ancient Polynesian names for this star were: *Kio Pa'a*[94] and *'Io Pa'a*, 'Io the immovable/steadfast/

unchanging. It was also known simply as *Kio* (Southern Polynesian dialect for ʻĪo) or *Kioio*.[95]

Ka Iwikuamoʻo (The Backbone) is a Polynesian Star (Line) Map that navigators (nā hoʻokele) on Polynesian canoes would use to navigate throughout Polynesia. This Star Map anciently began with *ʻĪo Paʻa*, The North Star and ended with the star cluster known anciently as *Hōkūkeʻa*, the Cross Star, or *Hānai-a-ka-Malama*, Adopted by the Light. Is this a coincidence? Let the reader decide.

The North Star - Ancient Names
ʻIopaʻa, Kiopaʻa, Kioʻio
Represents
ʻĪo, The Supreme God
Unchanging, Immovable
It is the only star that does not move. All the other stars in the heavens revolve around it.

Ka Iwikuamoʻo
The Ancient Navigational "Backbone"
Of Polynesia
Begins with the Supreme Creator God and ends in the Cross

Big Dipper/Nā Hiku
The Seven

The "Star of Gladness" that marks Hawaiʻi
Arcturus/Hōkūleʻa

Leo

Spica
ancient name
Hikiau
"I am Coming"

Corvus
ancient name
Kameʻe
"The Hero"

The Southern Cross - Ancient Names
Hōkūkeʻa - Cross Star
Hānai a ka Malama - Adopted by the Light

Nā Kuhikuhi/The Pointers

## The Maori and the God of the Bible

Because 'Io was so uncannily like the Hebrew God Yahweh, some foreign historians believed that the Maori 'Io had evolved after contact with Christian teaching. However, there are references to 'Io in the literature of different Maori tribes well before the Old Testament was introduced to New Zealand.[96]

*Elsmore* wrote, when European missionaries began to spread over New Zealand, they encountered groups of *"Christian"* Maori, none of whom they had established.[97] In *Poneke* (Wellington) they found that *"Christian"* prayers were already being offered.

In 1852, the Rev. *Richard Taylor* wrote, *"Io, the great God of Waikato and Ngati Kahungunu. The resemblance of His name to Ihowa was pointed out to me by the natives themselves, who still affirm it to be the ancient name of this God. They say He was the Maker of heaven and earth and the first man."*[98]

A kaumatua of *Ngati Hikairo* said in an interview that they continued in the sacred and secret ritual of the sacrifice of the lamb. It symbolized the faith of the ancestor of Tainui in the spiritual links between Earth and Heaven and man and Jehovah. It was a discipline practiced and brought by the ancestors to Aotearoa on the Tainui canoe. When the teachings of the Bible came, Jehovah and his Ten Commandments were embraced by the Maori and the ritual re-sanctified based upon Genesis in the Bible.[99]

The following are portions of a translated Maori sacred chant of creation compared to Genesis 1.

*"Io dwelt within the breathing space of immensity. The universe was in darkness, with water everywhere. There was no glimmer of dawn, no clearness, no light. And he*

*began by saying these words, that he might cease remaining inactive, 'Darkness, become a light-possessing darkness.' And at once light appeared."*[100]

Genesis 1:2-3 KJV says, *"And the earth was without form, and void; and darkness was upon the face of the deep. And the Spirit of God moved upon the face of the waters. And God said, Let there be light: and there was light."*. . .

*"Io then looked to the waters which compassed him about and spake a fourth time, saying, 'Ye waters of Tai-kama, be ye separate. Heaven be formed. 'Then the sky became suspended. 'Bring forth thou Tupu-horo-nuku.' And at once the moving earth lay stretched abroad."*[101]

Genesis 1:6-9 KJV, *"And God said, Let there be a firmament in the midst of the waters, and let it divide the waters from the waters. And God made the firmament, and divided the waters which were under the firmament from the waters which were above the firmament: and it was so. And God called the firmament Heaven. And the evening and the morning were the second day. And God said, Let the waters under the heaven be gathered together unto one place, and let the dry land appear: and it was so."*

*Peter Buck* counted 27 different names for 'Io.[102] A few of these names and their meanings, listed below, are compared with Biblical descriptions of God.

*Io-matua*: he is the parent of all things, natural phenomena, plants, animals, man, and gods.

Colossians 1:16 KJV "For by him were all things created, that are in heaven, and that are in earth, visible and invisible"

*Io-matua-kore*: He had no parents, "He was nothing but himself." He always existed.

(Hebrew) Yahweh: meaning. The Self- existent One. Exodus 3:14, "I AM THAT I AM."

*Io-te-wananga*: He is the source of all knowledge.

Colossians 2:3 KJV "In whom are hid all the treasures of wisdom and knowledge."

*Io-mata-ngaro*: His face is hidden and unseen.

Exodus 33:20 KJV, "And he said, Thou canst not see my face: for there shall no man see me, and live."

*Io-te-waiora*: He is the source and giver of life.

Psalm 36:9 KJV, "For with thee is the fountain of life:"

*Io-mata-wai*: 'Io, the God of love.

John 3:16 KJV, "For God so loved the world, that he gave his only begotten Son, that whosoever believeth in him should not perish, but have everlasting life."

## The Maori Kings, the Bible and 'Io

The content of this portion of the book is by permission of the Maori Kingitanga (Maori King's Office)

The first two Maori Kings, *Potatau* and *Tawhiao*, were Grand priests of the 'Io religion, the highest degree in the *Tainui* priesthood of 'Io. There are no priests of that rank anymore. In this religion, there was one supreme God, 'Io, who sang the universe into being. 'Io was so sacred that ordinary humans did not have access to him. Like the Hebrew God, *Yahweh*, even uttering his name was avoided.

This next section contains information from the books *Tawhiao-King or Prophet* and *Koroki My King*.[103]

King Potatau believed that there can be only one Creator God so the Creator God the missionaries taught must be the same God of the Maori. Potatau could not share the *tapu* (sacred) secrets of the *Ware Wananga* (Sacred House of

Learning) with the common people, but the knowledge of Christianity was *noa* (free) for all. Potatau welcomed and encouraged the missionaries. He told his people that the Bible was a treasure that comes from heaven and could not be bought but was offered freely in the light of day.

King Tawhiao

The book, *Tawhiao – King or Prophet*, states that King Tawhiao, looked into the remote past to the Beginning of All with the Supreme Being. Like queen *Lili'uokalani*, his father, the first king, Potatau, saw much good in the teachings of Jehovah from the genuine missionaries although later *"missionaries"* wanted the land. Tawhiao wasn't educated by missionaries but his father, Potatau, ensured that Tawhiao communicated with Jehovah and still continued to keep the 'Īo teaching of the Ware Wananga. When Potatau and Tawhiao heard the Bible preached, they said there was nothing they heard that was against what they knew of 'Īo. They both accepted *Ihu Karaiti* (Jesus Christ) and wanted all of their people to accept Ihu Karaiti. The way to approach 'Īo was in a very *"Old Testament"* way. Very difficult and with much protocol. If you were not the right person or came before 'Īo at the wrong place or time, it could be death. The way to 'Īo was very Tapu (Kapu – Sacred and restricted). However, Ihu Karaiti made the way to 'Īo *"noa"*. Tawhiao was the first baptized King. The flag raised at his coronation displays the cross prominently at the top.

In the book, *Tawhiao – King or Prophet*, several important statements are made. It states that, the *kaumatua* (The Elders they interviewed for the book) would ask themselves why did Tawhiao readily embrace the Word (the Bible). They concluded that the "*old people*" were already hungering for it. Their kaumatua told them the King did not study the Bible but the verses he cherished and quoted so often came direct to him from 'Io. They said a favorite verse of Tawhiao was: "*Blessed are the meek: for they will inherit the earth.*" The kaumatua of Tawhiao's tribe, Tainui of the Waikato said that King Tawhiao was a man of God and a righteous King as "*'Io Matua Kore ('Io the Parentless) is King of Kings.*" Tawhiao wanted his people to stop "*makutu*" (Maori witchcraft) and just follow Ihu Karaiti, Jesus Christ. 'Io and Jehovah were the same God to King Tawhiao.

This Coat of Arms of the Kingitanga, commissioned by King Tawhiao, reflects his belief in 'Io and Jesus. Tawhiao commissioned two Tohunga of the 'Io religion to create this Coat of Arms. The cross is the centerpiece of the Coat of Arms.

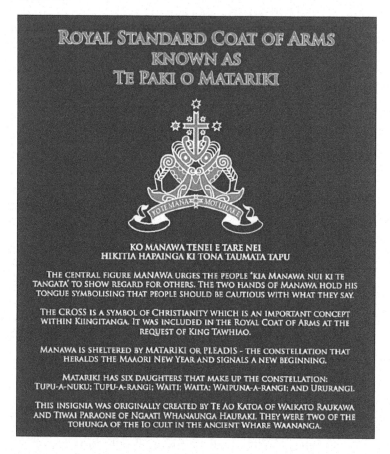

ROYAL STANDARD COAT OF ARMS
KNOWN AS
TE PAKI O MATARIKI

KO MANAWA TENEI E TARE NEI
HIKITIA HAPAINGA KI TONA TAUMATA TAPU

THE CENTRAL FIGURE MANAWA URGES THE PEOPLE 'KIA MANAWA NUI KI TE TANGATA' TO SHOW REGARD FOR OTHERS. THE TWO HANDS OF MANAWA HOLD HIS TONGUE SYMBOLISING THAT PEOPLE SHOULD BE CAUTIOUS WITH WHAT THEY SAY.

THE CROSS IS A SYMBOL OF CHRISTIANITY WHICH IS AN IMPORTANT CONCEPT WITHIN KIINGITANGA. IT WAS INCLUDED IN THE ROYAL COAT OF ARMS AT THE REQUEST OF KING TAWHIAO.

MANAWA IS SHELTERED BY MATARIKI OR PLEADIS - THE CONSTELLATION THAT HERALDS THE MAAORI NEW YEAR AND SIGNALS A NEW BEGINNING.

MATARIKI HAS SIX DAUGHTERS THAT MAKE UP THE CONSTELLATION: TUPU-A-NUKU; TUPU-A-RANGI; WAITI; WAITA; WAIPUNA-A-RANGI; AND URURANGI.

THIS INSIGNIA WAS ORIGINALLY CREATED BY TE AO KATOA OF WAIKATO RAUKAWA AND TIWAI PARAONE OF NGAATI WHANAUNGA HAURAKI. THEY WERE TWO OF THE TOHUNGA OF THE IO CULT IN THE ANCIENT WHARE WAANANGA.

The Maori King's crown is the Bible. "*Ko te mea mīharo o roto i tēnei karaunatanga a te tangata Māori i tō tāua nei kīngi, kāore i whakawahia ki te hinu, engari he mea hoatu he Paipera ki runga i tōna **māhunga** (TP 11/1912:6). / The amazing thing of this coronation of a*

*Māori of our king was that he wasn't anointed with oil but a Bible was placed on his head."* (maoridictionary.co.nz)

From teara.govt.nz, *"The ceremony itself is simple and impressive. It begins when the King-elect, who wears Potatau's coronation korowai (mantle-cloak), is escorted to a point facing on to the marae. Three sides of this are lined by those who have come to pay their last respects to the late King while, by the fourth side, near where the King-elect stands with the principal chiefs of the King tribes, is an open tent containing the late King's coffin. The proceedings are all in Maori. A clergyman first recites the preliminary portions of the Anglican service and preaches a sermon. When this is over the senior descendant of Wiremu Tamihana Te Waharoa* (Wiremu, called the Maori "Kingmaker" coronated the first King, Potatau and the second king, Tawhiao.) *steps forward to stand facing the King-elect. He then crowns the King by laying a Bible upon his head, saying as he does so, "Your ancestors in the olden days were wont to be anointed with oil, but, since the advent of Christianity, they have been anointed with the Word of God. Therefore I place the Word of God upon your head". Te Waharoa then leads the "King" forward, declaring him to be "King of the Maori race, in the Name of the Father, and of the Son, and of the Holy Ghost".*

From the first Maori King, Potatau, until today's King, Tuheitia, the same Bible has been used in the coronation ceremony to crown the new King or Queen.

At the coronation ceremony of Kingi Tuheitia, Maori Bishop Kito Pikaahu said, *"The crown that you wear, is not a crown of diamonds, gold or silver. It is the crown of the Bible, the living Word of God, the Holy Word of God."* (episcopalnewsservice.org)

## Kauikeaouli, Kamehameha III

Memorial at the birthplace of Kauikeaouli, Keauhou Bay

*Kauikeaouli* was the second son born to Kamehameha the Great and his sacred wife Keʻōpūolani. Both of his parents knew of 'Io (Because descendants of both know of 'Io). He was born at *Keauhou* (meaning: The New Era) Bay, island of Hawaiʻi. An enclosure there holds the stone he was laid on when he was born and a plaque commemorates his birth. However, Kauikeaouli was stillborn. The historian Kamakau, in *"Ka Moolelo O Na Kamehameha,"* the original Hawaiian language newspaper version of the book, *Ruling Chiefs*, says twice that the child *"make,"* was dead and also says that the chief Kuakini did not want the child's corpse (*kupapaʻu*). The child was, as we say in pidgin Hawaiian, *"make, die, dead,"* really dead. As stated in the introduction to this book, all historians are subjective, none are totally objective. We all translate what we see, read or hear through the lens of what we believe. Although Kamakau said the child was really dead, a corpse, every secular translator to English wrote, *"The child seemed stillborn."* Apparently, they changed what Kamakau wrote and added in *"seemed,"* to comply with their belief that no person can be raised from the dead. Because I believe Jesus was raised from the dead and I know personally several people who have been raised from the dead (Including 2 Hawaiians and a First Nations Canadian chief), I have a different point of view.

The narrative continues that then came the kāula, Kapihe, who had given the prophecy, *"The ancient kapu will be overthrown, the heiau and lele altars will be overthrown, and the images will fall down. God will be in the heavens; the Islands will unite, the chiefs will fall, and those of the earth (the lesser people) will rise,"* from about two miles away *(near Kuamo'o).* This means the child was dead for a long time as this area is rough 'a'ā lava fields difficult to walk on. Kapihe was coming to meet the new heir with his ali'i and entourage. When they were told that the child was dead, Kapihe replied, *"The child is not dead, life will come to him."* All the English translators write, *"The child will not die, he will live."* Kapihe was from the Napua line of kāhuna descended from Makua-kau-mana whose god was Ka-'onohi-o-ka-la (similar to the child of God). This incident took place in 1814, about 6 years before the missionaries arrived. Kapihe fanned the corpse, sprinkled it with water, and at the same time recited a prayer addressed to the Child of God. Kapihe prayed:

*"The heavens lighten with the God,*
*The earth burns with the Child,*

"*O Son, pour down the rain that brings the rainbow,*
(When the missionaries arrived Hewahewa chanted, "*A rainbow standing in the ocean, Is Jesus, Our Redeemer.*" Hawaiians thought a standing rainbow was the sign that a god was there.)
*There in heaven is the Lord.*
*Life flows through my spirit,*
*Dedicated to your law.*"

Kauikeaouli began to move, make sounds and came to life. Kapihe gave the child the name, Ke-aweawe-ʻula, "*The red trail,*" signifying the pathway by which the God descends from the heavens.[104]

In 1825, when Kauikeaouli was between ten and eleven years old, he became king. At this time, the young King proclaimed to the chiefs and people gathered for his coronation, "*My kingdom I give to God.*" God was, therefore, made the ruler of the Hawaiian Kingdom and "*Keauhou,*" the New Era began, the Christian Kingdom of Hawaiʻi.

As he grew into a young adult, like many young men, Kauikeaouli rebelled against Christian morality and the over strict, unbiblical rules the missionaries imposed on the people; like no dancing, playing games, surfing and showing public affection. The Bible says that King David danced before the Lord with all his might. The Hawaiian Bible uses the word "*ha'a*" for "*dance*." Ha'a is an ancient hula form and yet hula was forbidden. Four times the Bible says to greet one another with a "holy kiss." Yet on the voyage to Hawai'i, one of the young missionary couples was confronted by the others for practicing the "*most sickening familiarity*" in the cabin and on deck. They were charged with "*holding hands, kissing each other, and openly demonstrating affection in public, thus flagrantly and sinfully corrupting the morals of missionary children and heathen.*"[105]

However, the laws against adultery, gambling and alcohol would help to protect the Hawaiian people. Sexually transmitted diseases were decimating his people and many Hawaiians later lost their lands while gambling and/or signed their lands over to others when drunk.

Later in life, Kauikeaouli did return to his Christian faith in spite of the flaws of the missionaries. He signed the constitution of 1840 which affirmed the statement he made at his coronation, "*My kingdom I give to God.*" This constitution says, "*God hath made of one blood all nations of men to dwell on the earth, in unity and blessedness. God has also bestowed certain rights alike on all men and all chiefs, and all people of all lands.*

*These are some of the rights which He has given alike to every man and every chief of correct deportment; life, limb, and liberty, freedom from oppression; the earnings of his hands and the productions of his mind, not however to those who act in violation of the laws.*

*God has also established government, and rule for the purpose of peace; but in making laws for the nation it is by no means proper to enact laws for the protection of the rulers only, without also providing protection for their subjects; neither is it proper to enact laws to enrich the chiefs only, without regard to enriching their subjects also, and hereafter there shall by no means be any laws enacted which are at variance with what is above expressed, neither shall any tax be assessed, nor any service or labor required of any man, in a manner which is at variance with the above sentiments...no chief may be able to oppress any subject, but that chiefs and people may enjoy the same protection, under one and the same law.*

How different this law was from the laws of the kapu system that had taxed the common people into poverty, used them for slave labor and called for a makaʻinana (commoner) child to be strangled on the altar of a heiau for the sin of chiefess Kapiʻolani of eating a banana. The Constitution continued: "*It is our design to regulate our kingdom according to the above principles and thus seek the greatest prosperity both of all the chiefs and all of the people of these Hawaiian Islands. But we are aware that we cannot ourselves alone accomplish such an object - God must be our aid, for it is His province alone to give perfect protection and prosperity. - Wherefore we first present our supplication to HIM, that he will guide us to right measures and sustain us in our work.*

*It is therefore our fixed decree,*

I.  *That no law shall be enacted which is at variance with the word of the Lord Jehovah or at variance with the general spirit of His word. All laws of the Islands shall be in consistency with the general spirit of God's law.*"[106]

When the Hawaiian Kingdom was seized in 1843 by the British, Great Britain was the most powerful nation in the world. Kauikeaouli asked the people to pray. When the Kingdom was returned, the King thanked God at Kawaiahahaʻo Church and spoke what is now our State motto, *"Ua mau ke ea o ka ʻāina i ka pono," "The life of the land is perpetuated in righteousness."* This legacy, to care for the people and the land in righteousness, was given to Kauikeaouli by his mother, the highest aliʻi in the land and the first to be baptized, Keʻōpūolani. On her deathbed, she passed this legacy to her sons, Liholiho (Kamehameha II) and Kauikeaouli.[107]

Kauikeauoli Kamehameha III

Keʻōpūolani said to her sons, *"Take care of these lands which you have received from your father. Exercise a tender care over the people. Protect the missionaries, and be kind to them. Walk in the straight path. Keep the Sabbath. Serve God. Love him, and love Jesus Christ."*[108] Therefore, the righteousness Kauikeaouli was speaking of was the righteousness of Jesus Christ.

133

Despite many trials and much adversity, the Kingdom prospered during Kauikeaouli's reign. In 1844 agreements were made with the United States, Great Britain and France that recognized the Hawaiian Kingdom as an independent nation. Hawai'i became the first non-white member of the *"family of nations"* (Which later became the *"League of Nations"* and then the *"United Nations"*). This was because Hawaii was an educated Christian nation. Kauikeaouli was the longest reigning Hawaiian monarch, ruling 29 years.

# Chapter 13

# Why the Rejection of 'Io and His Connection to the God of the Bible?

When we began Aloha Ke Akua in 1993, a Word was given to me in prayer that there were "*three cords*" binding the Hawaiian people from "**coming home**" to 'Io who is their God and the same as the God of the Bible.

## The Three Stranded Cord of Rejection

**Cord One**: The Hawaiian people see the God of the Bible as a foreign God, not Our God.

It was time again for the Hawaiian people to remember the name of their true God, 'Io. And that 'Io, the One Creator God of Hawai'i and the One Creator God of the Bible are One and the same. This separation of the Creator God of the Hawaiian people and the Creator God of the Bible has caused much confusion in the hearts of many Hawaiians from the time the missionaries arrived until today.

This separation was also caused by unbiblical doctrine that was taught to the Hawaiian people about the God of the Bible. They were taught that they never knew this God even though Romans 1:20 NIV says, *"For since the creation of the world God's invisible qualities—his eternal power and divine nature—have been clearly seen, being understood from what has been made, so that people are without excuse."* The Bible clearly says that all people knew the Creator God. Therefore, if the Bible is true, the Hawaiian people knew the Creator God. In all of Polynesia, there is only one God that matches the nature of the God of the Bible, ʻĪo.

Missionary preaching at Waimea Valley
Hewahewa was said to be in attendance

Other un-Biblical doctrines were taught. For instance, Hewahewa had applied to the missionaries for baptism. However, they turned him down after they heard from John Young that he had supervised the sacrificing of 13 Ka'ū high chiefs at the dedication of *Pu'ukohola* Heiau in 1791. The Bible tells us that the sacrifice of Jesus is powerful enough to cleanse us of all sins. It is Jewish tradition that the Apostle Paul had supervised the killing of thousands of Jews. Paul was forgiven of his sins but Hewahewa was not. Disillusioned, Hewahewa eventually retired from public life and activity in the church. When some of the missionaries heard that he had become inactive in church attendance, they labeled him a *"backslider."* They said he had returned to his drunken *"heathen"* ways and was worshipping at his family heiau. Yet, it is also written in the missionary journal, *The Friend*, that *"He lived in the valley of Waimea, a faithful, consistent follower of the new light."* (The Friend, March 1, 1914). Which is true and which propaganda? Descendants of the family of Hewahewa have recorded what their kūpuna, who knew Hewahewa, told them about his nature. Their kūpuna attest that he loved his God, was a Christian and taught them to keep Christian ways. Hewahewa wanted a Christian burial instead of a burial like his ancestors.[109] It seems that Hewahewa was confused because what the Bible taught and what the missionaries taught was different. When Hewahewa was nearing death, he asked one of his relatives to pray continuously for him. He was afraid to die because of his sins. How sad that at the end of his life, Hewahewa, was not sure if his sins were forgiven. The forgiveness of sins was the reason Jesus came and died. It is the foundation stone of Christianity.

The harsh, unforgiving God that was taught to Queen Lili'uokalani by her missionary teachers also caused confusion in her heart. It was not the God she read about in the Bible or met in her personal prayer time. It was not the God of Aloha she knew who could make "*scarlet sins white in an instant*".[110] Lili'uokalani believed in the God embodied in the "*Spirit of Aloha*," God as Love, Grace (unmerited favor), Mercy and Forgiveness, despite the missionaries' teaching of a vengeful and unforgiving God. She had a Romans 1:20 relationship with her God, the one she could see in the natural beauty of her islands. She sometimes missed church and as her diary states, "*I spent the day in the woods in the silence with the One we have been taught to fear. I feel His presence.*"[111] During the time of the overthrow of the queen, many Hawaiians returned to the old gods because the God of the Bible seemed to favor the foreigners who did not follow the Bible. Even through this confusion, when the Queen was offered help from a kahuna and the old gods she said, "*I told him the Bible was my only guide.*"[112] She remained a *Follower of Jesus* through the wrongful overthrow of her kingdom by people calling themselves "Christians (Followers of Christ)." Evidently, because she trusted the Bible and her personal relationship with her God more than the un-Christlike behavior of those claiming to be "following after Christ." She would daily spend time in prayer, reading and meditating on the "*Word of God*."[113] Lili'uokalani knew Bible scripture well and would typically hold Bible Study every morning for her household retainers. Her favorite scripture helped her to live Aloha towards her tormentors "*Forgive us our trespasses as we forgive those who trespass against us*," which she would compare to an old Hawaiian proverb, "*No one is free from their own sin until they have forgiven those who have sinned against them*."[114]

Lili'uokalani was accused of being a sorceress, sacrificing a pig (Which her diary said was killed for a birthday luau) and worshipping Pele (Even though it was she who asked the churches to pray to God when lava threatened Hilo in 1881). In reply she wrote, "*Perhaps I have 'indulged' in harmless 'superstitions' of our native customs in hoping to preserve some of our old traditions. Never the less, while the missionaries have ornamented their Christmas Trees we have never called them Druids*."[115] Christmas Trees are not a Christian tradition but a "*pagan*" European one.

Could many of the mixed reports about Lili'uokalani and Hewahewa be attributed to their worshipping in Hawaiian cultural ways a God that the Bible attests they knew (Rom. 1:20) and the ethnocentric propaganda of foreign Christians?

Te Whatahoro, the last 'Io high priest of the East Coast Maori said, "*If the early missionaries had learned of and studied the cult of Io, and had not so despised our religion, I think that the cult would have been incorporated with Christianity and would now be a part of the Bible*."[116]

A news article from New Zealand, 1939, stated *"The highest grade of Maori religion before the arrival of the missionaries was a beautiful conception with high ethics and one God very similar in many ways to the Christian religion, but these were unfortunately unknown to the missionaries, who regarded the Maori as an uncivilized being whose religion and ideas were all evil. They attempted to break up these old and beautiful beliefs to make room for their Christian teachings. The result was simply to confuse the mind of the Maori. Old religions and beliefs do not die out easily, and at the back of the Maori's mind there was always the idea that his old beliefs were not as wrong as they were painted."*[117]

I think Romans 1:20 needs to be reiterated, *"For since the creation of the world God's invisible qualities, his eternal power and divine nature, have been clearly seen, being understood from what has been made, so that people are without excuse."* NIV

The Apostle Paul, speaking to the Areopagus, the highest counsel of Athens, said in Acts 17:26-28 NIV *"From one man he (God) made all the nations, that they should inhabit the whole earth; and he marked out their appointed times in history and the boundaries of their lands. God did this so that they would seek him and perhaps reach out for him and find him, though he is not far from any one of us. 'For in him we live and move and have our being.' As some of your own poets have said, 'We are his offspring.'"*

It would be un-Biblical if the Hawaiian people had nothing in their culture that reflected their relationship with their Creator God.

**Cord Two:** The Rejection of the Hawaiian Culture as Evil and of the Devil

God created much beauty and gave many important gifts to His Hawaiian children in the culture He created. The culture just needs to be returned to the worship of 'Io. For instance, in 1993, when we started Aloha Ke Akua, no hula was allowed in church. Hula is like any vehicle of expression (language, music, poetry, dance, painting, sculpture, etc.), it is just a vehicle to express the heart, mind, emotions and thoughts of the person using the vehicle. If someone drives a car drunk and kills someone, is their car put in prison? Neither is a vehicle of expression good or bad but an expression of the one *"driving"* it. Hula is the language of the Hawaiian people.

King Kalākaua loved his culture. Like all the Hawaiian royalty, he grew up in the Christian school where he learned that his culture was of the devil. This tore his heart apart like it did many of the ali'i and many Hawaiians until today. Hawaiians love their culture but were taught that their culture was sinful by misguided missionaries. Of the hula Kalākaua said, *"Hula is the language of the heart, and therefore the heartbeat of the Hawaiian people."* Hula could not be danced for the Christian God, so he restored it with worship of other gods. Yet, Kalākaua was baptized in the Anglican Church in 1863.[118] This confusion is still carried on in the hearts of many Hawaiians today.

**Cord Three:** People calling themselves *"Christians"* but not following Christ have hurt the Hawaiian people.

It is important to remember that just because someone sits in church and calls himself a *"Christian"* doesn't make him a Christian (**A Follower of Jesus**).

It is also important to remember that the missionaries did not fulfill the Hawaiian prophecies of the return of *Ke Akua Maoli*, the True God, in His new form. The coming of this God was fulfilled in the Book the missionaries brought that told about Iesū. The first missionaries, although flawed as humans are, left without a penny in their pockets or died here with nothing, having given their lives for the Hawaiian people. Queen Lili'uokalani was careful to distinguish between the *"Missionary (Political) Party"* and the true missionaries to whom she attributed much good.[119]

The Mission Board required their missionaries to follow specific and explicit rules that **barred them from involvement and interference in the affairs of this world. They were not to take up positions in government or to do any business transactions or take any employment for personal gain. All business transactions and all employment had to be approved by the other missionaries and all monies earned were to be turned over to the mission. Missionaries could get involved in worldly affairs only if they resigned from the Mission.**[120]

The Hawaiian mission ended in 1863. The overthrow of the Hawaiian Kingdom happened in 1893, 30 years later, by members of the Political Party that was unfortunately called the *"Missionary Party."* There were no missionaries in Hawai'i in 1893 and no missionaries were involved in the overthrow of the Queen. The overthrowers were businessmen and plantation owners. However, some of the overthrowers were descendants of missionaries and all of them called themselves *"Christians."* All this has caused much confusion because of propaganda and the compression of history over time.

If people who called themselves *"Christians"* lied, stole, cheated and took advantage of people to build a kingdom in this world of land, money and power; they were not following Jesus. **Jesus would have never done that**. Jesus said his kingdom was not of this world. The kepalo (the devil) offered him all the kingdoms of this world and Iesū refused. Iesū didn't even have a home. People calling themselves Christians but not following Iesū have caused much confusion for many Hawaiians and caused many Hawaiians to reject Iesū.

The rejection of the God of the Bible is very understandable when people who called themselves Christians made statements like the following:

*"I have an exalted idea of the destiny of the white man and of his power to control and govern both men and elements."*[121]

The San Francisco Examiner wrote of the sorcery of a black, savage, pagan queen that was causing extreme danger to the white population of Hawaiʻi.[122]

(The following quotes are from a paper called, *"To Raise A Voice in Praise"* by Dr. Ron Williams)

*"We do not want higher education at all in the Kamehameha Schools. Provision for that will be made in other ways in exceptional cases. The average Hawaiian has no such capacity."*

"A Wonderful Week." *"...most dramatic of the series came the tragic, scenic, self-murder of the monarchy:*

*when, encouraged by kāhunas, the half-maddened Queen broke her oath, and discarded the Constitution* (This was the Bayonet Constitution that was forced upon King Kalākaua by White businessmen and put the power of government in their hands.[123]), *to the horror of her white partisans, and to the exulting hope of the people she was betraying, who now saw clear the way to cast off the incubus of her caprice and arrogance which they had so wearily and patiently endured. At once sprang forth the wrath and power of the conservative and long suffering whites."*

An article in *The Friend* in the February 1895 issue entitled *A Manifest Divine Protection* stated that while an important reason for the new government's victory was the *"vastly superior courage and prowess of the white man in battle with those of a weaker race, the devout should know that the success of the white leaders over the Natives was 'the merciful gift of the Divine Protector,' who 'teacheth our hands to war and our fingers to fight."*

We have much of this information thanks to what has been called the *"Third Wave of Hawaiian Historians."* Of whom, Dr. Ron Williams is prominent.

Many Hawaiians also were angry at Hawaiian Christians because of the propaganda in the English language newspapers which claimed that most Hawaiian Christians wanted the Queen overthrown and their nation to become a part of the United States. However, because of the *"Third Wave Historians"* who are studying the Hawaiian Language Newspapers, we now know that the vast majority of Hawaiian Christians were in support of and praying for the restoration of the Queen.

## A Foreign Bowl

The Gospel, *"The Good News of Jesus,"* was not good news to many because of the above three cords. The Gospel was brought in a bowl of foreign soil and never was allowed to grow roots deep into the native soil of Hawai'i. Whenever roots of the Gospel tried to come out of the bowl and plant itself on native soil, they were cut off by the *"Christian"* teachers. The parable of the Sower and the Seed says, *"Some fell on rocky places, where it did not have much soil. It sprang up quickly, because the soil was shallow. But when the sun came up, the plants were scorched, and they withered because they had no root* (Mat. 13:5-6)." Similarly, because the Gospel was kept in the shallow bowl of foreign soil and had no deep roots into the native soil, when trials came, it died away because there were no deep roots. The God of the Bible was not "Our God" or the *Gospel*, *"Good News."* Thus, while during the reign of King Kauikeaouli (mid-1800s) 96% of Hawaiians were Christians, the vast majority of Hawaiians left the church after the overthrow of Queen Lili'uokalani, and angrily rebelled against Christ in the 1970s through the 1990s. Many today (2021) still harbor this anger and rebellion against Christ.

A friend wrote to me, *"In the 1970s, thirty years ago, my late grandmother (Kahuaka'inui Umuiwi) was irritated by young Hawaiians who honored the gods of the past and spoke negatively of the missionaries. She said, 'When they say that our people blindly followed the missionaries, they are calling their kupuna 'stupid.' Our grandparents were not stupid when they became Christians. They knew what it was to live a life of fear. The old religion was all about fear. They knew what they were doing when they turned*

145

to the God of the Bible. They turned from fear to a God of love and freedom from fear."

The Kūpuna of the early 1900s who were told by their Kūpuna what it was like to live under the Kapu System would never return to the terror and bondage of that system. Some younger Hawaiians today, because of their anger against "Christians" who were not following Christ, want to view the Kapu System through "rose-colored" glasses and return to it. This is impossible as will be explained in the next chapter.

In the book, "*Pagan Christianity*," which is about American Christianity, we find that American Christianity is mostly cultural and not scriptural. American Christians do not think they accepted a foreign Jewish religion and a foreign Jewish God. This God and Christianity have become so much a part of American culture, "*It is ours.*" To many Hawaiians, Christianity is still the foreign religion of the foreign God.

The *Gospel*, the Good News, is that Iesū came to restore our relationship with our Creator. The God of the Bible does not ask a person to be like any other person or to change his personality; a person is just to change the focus of his life from other gods to the OneTrue God. He does not ask people to change from one "*sin stained*" culture to another; just to rededicate their culture to Him.

# Chapter 14

# The Importance of ʻĪo to the Hawaiian People (Reprise)

If the Creator God of the Hawaiian people is different than the Creator God of the Bible, then the God of the Bible is a foreign God, not "Our God." He is a God who lived with His favored children and will only accept us if we become like His favored children. This is not Aloha. It is Aloha if this God lovingly created us, guided us to these islands and has been with us from the beginning. It is Aloha if He loved us even when we left Him for other gods. It is Aloha if He forgives us for turning to other gods and sacrificing His beloved Hawaiian people, made in His image, in worship to these gods. It is Aloha if He sacrificed Himself in the person of Iesū, so that we could return home to Him. This is a God of Aloha.

Many Hawaiians, because of their justifiable anger against the actions and teaching of some who called them-selves "*Christians*," reject Christianity. They love their culture and desire a Hawaiian religion. However, this is not possible without returning to 'Io. If one wants to be authentic to the culture and religion of the Kapu System, then one must kill himself/herself because all have eaten together, men and women. There was no grace or mercy. If one takes only parts of this religion and culture, he/she is not being authentic but creating a new religion and culture. The foundation of the Kapu System was the Kapu, the breaking of which led to death. To be authentic to this religion and culture, the death penalty for breaking Kapu needs to be reinstated.

Therefore, the only choice to being an authentic Hawaiian is to return to 'Io. A religion when people were sacred to 'Io and not to be killed. A culture where the ali'i were close to the common people like parents. It is true that very little of this religion and culture remains and that much of what remains has been tainted by the religion and culture of the Kapu System.

However, my kūpuna and mentors taught me that we can use two things as our guide to the original nature of this culture: True Aloha, what is now referred to as **Kapu** (as in sacred/holy) **Aloha** and the Bible.

***Kapu*** - *Holy/Sacred*, ***Aloha*** = ***Alo*** – *In the Presence of*, ***Hā*** – *The Sacred Breath/Spirit of Life*. When we call for Kapu Aloha, we are calling for the Holy Spirit of God to be with us.

## Aloha

Aloha is:

"*Akahai*" – Tender Kindness

"*Lōkahi*" – Unity in harmony and peace

"*Oluʻolu*" – Graciousness (as in unmerited favor and
   forgiveness)
"*Haʻahaʻa*" – Humility
"*Ahonui*" – Patience and Long suffering

This description of Aloha was given by Pilahi Paki,
who was one of the most respected and beloved kupuna
(deceased), known for her Aloha and her knowledge of
Hawaiian culture. All of these words describing "*Aloha*"
are aspects of Love. Aloha is the embodiment of perfect
Love. These descriptions of Aloha cannot be accomplished
without mercy, empathy, grace (unmerited favor), forgiveness and compassion; which are all aspects of Aloha.
Aloha is so deeply spiritual that all of these words still do
not do it justice.

All of these descriptions of Aloha cannot be achieved
without forgiveness. In the old days of Hawaiʻi, when the
sacredness of "*Aloha*" was understood, one could not even
speak the word, "*Aloha*," if there was any hate, bitterness,
anger or unforgiveness in one's heart. One would have
to cleanse oneself before even speaking the sacred word,
"*Aloha*."

Queen Liliʻuokalani's favorite scripture was, "(God)
*Forgive us our trespasses, as we forgive those who tres-
pass against us.*" She would compare this scripture with
an old Hawaiian proverb, "*No one is free from their own
sin, until they have forgiven those who have sinned against
them.*" The Queen knew that not forgiving is like drinking
poison and hoping the other person dies. Unforgiveness
causes bitterness, hatred, anger, frustration, vengefulness
and hurt in one's life. This often leads to family abuse,
alcohol and drug abuse, health problems and suicide. Ka

Bibala, the Bible says, "*See to it that no one falls short of the grace of God and that no bitter root grows up to cause trouble and defile many.*" Hebrews 12:15. I was taught by my kūpuna and mentors that you either Aloha or you don't Aloha. You cannot Aloha some and not others, you must Aloha everyone. You can hate what people do but you must Aloha them. If you hate some, it will cause your na'au (heart/soul) to become bitter and dark. The bitterness and darkness will spread throughout your life and to one's family and friends. Aloha cannot survive in darkness because "Aloha Ke Akua," God is Aloha and God is Light. If one is a warrior of unforgiveness, bitterness, anger and vengefulness, one will be destroyed by the darkness. When we pass this hatred, unforgiveness, bitterness, anger and vengefulness onto our nā keiki (children), we perpetuate the darkness and the destruction of our people. If a person is a warrior of Aloha who fights for what is pono (righteous) because of his/her Aloha for our people, the 'āina, and the future of our keiki; he/she is a warrior of the Light. He/She is a person who hates the evil people do but will Aloha them. Aloha and Maluhia (Peace) will be his/her portion.

Our Queen Lili'uokalani is my hero. To me, she is the personification of Aloha. Her kingdom was stolen by those in her church that she considered her friends and she was wrongly imprisoned in her own palace by them. Yet, while imprisoned, she wrote the mele (song) that is now known as *The Queen's Prayer*, *Ke Aloha O Ka Haku* (The Love of the Lord).

# The Queen's Prayer

| Ke Aloha O Ka Haku | The Love of the Lord |
|---|---|
| ʻO kou aloha nō | Your loving mercy |
| Aia i ka lani, | Is as high as Heaven |
| A ʻo kou ʻoiāʻiʻo | And your truth |
| Hemolele hoʻi | So perfect |
| | |
| Koʻu noho mihi ʻana | I live in sorrow |
| A paʻahao ʻia | Imprisoned |
| ʻO ʻoe kuʻu lama | You are my light |
| Kou nani koʻu koʻo | Your glory, my support |
| | |
| Mai nānā ʻino ʻino | Behold not with malevolence |
| Nā hewa o kānaka | The sins of man |
| Akā e huikala | But forgive |
| A maʻemaʻe nō | And cleanse |
| | |
| Nō Laila e ka Haku | And so, o Lord |
| Ma lalo o kouʻēheu | Protect us beneath your wings |
| Kō mākou maluhia | And let peace be our portion |
| A mau aku nō | Now and forever more |
| | |
| Amene | Amen |

Some may ask, "*If God is a loving God of Aloha, why did He allow all these bad things to happen to us?*" It is because God is a loving God of Aloha that He allows bad things to happen. God is All Powerful, He could force us to do anything He wants, but He did not want robots or slaves, but children to love. God is love, Aloha, and Aloha must be freely given, freely received, and freely returned. Aloha, by its very nature, cannot be forced on anyone.

Therefore, Ke Akua gave people the gift of the freedom to choose Aloha or evil. It is the gift that makes us children of God instead of slaves.

To those who have blamed God and been angry at Him, Ka Makua Lani, your Heavenly Father, is waiting for you, watching for you to come home. His Aloha for you is overflowing!

Joseph Nāwahī is another hero of mine. He was a true follower of Iesū and, he and his wife Emma are looked upon by many as the greatest Hawaiian patriots after our Queen. He was called a "Hawaiian Renaissance Man." He was a staunch supporter of the Queen and founded the Hui Aloha ʻĀina (People United in  their Love for the Land) Hawaiian Patriotic League. He also published and edited the Ke Aloha ʻĀina (The Love of the Land) Hawaiian language newspaper. Yet, through the overthrow of his Queen and the stealing of the Kingdom of Hawaiʻi by those claiming to be followers of Iesū, he recognized the difference between them and true follow- ers of Iesū. In an article attributed to Nāwahī entitled Ke Aloha ʻĀina printed in the Hawaiian language newspaper, Ka Leo O Ka Lahui, April 12, 1893, he says, "This gift created in man, that was intertwined into man when He (God) made man, is ALOHA (all in caps in the original Hawaiian newspaper article), and it is divided into three parts – 1. aloha Akua (love for God), 2. aloha kanaka (love for people), 3. aloha 'āina (love for the land). Therefore a person who truly aloha(s) these things surely must aloha all of them. And the person who says he has aloha 'āina (love for the land), and yet he denies God, his aloha is not real, profound, or true." In this article, Nāwahī exemplifies how a Hawaiian follower of Iesū can also be a "Hawaiian Renaissance Man" by using the Hawaiian precept of the Lokahi Triangle in his explanation of God's relationship with man.

Queen Lili'uokalani said, "*I could not turn back the time for the political change, but there is still time to save our heritage. You must remember never to cease to act because you fear you may fail. The way to lose any earthly kingdom is to be inflexible, intolerant, and prejudicial. Another way is to be too flexible, tolerant of too many wrongs, and without judgment at all. It is a razor's edge. It is the width of a blade of pili grass. To gain the kingdom of heaven is to hear what is not said, to see what cannot be seen, and to know the unknowable -- that is Aloha. All things in this world are two; in heaven there is but one.*"

Through Aloha, we can gain the kingdom of heaven on earth. "*Thy Kingdom come, thy will be done, on earth as it is in heaven* (The Lord's Prayer)." In this world, there is division, in heaven, all is Lōkahi (unity/harmony), the key to heaven on earth is Aloha.

It is interesting that, in the language Jesus spoke, Aramaic, the word for God is "*Aloha.*" "*The existing Aramaic and the Old Syriac manuscripts* (of the Bible) *use the word "Aloha"* (equivalent to the Hebrew Eloah, singular of Elohim), *as transliterated in the 1849 Etheridge version* (of the Bible) *for "God."* The new Gabriel Version of the Bible which translates the original Aramaic into English says of Jesus in John 1:1-4, "*In the beginning, the Word* (Jesus) *existed. The Word was with **Aloha**, and **Aloha** was the Word Himself [Aramaic]. He was with **Aloha** in the beginning. Everything was created by Him, and absolutely nothing came into existence without Him. In Him was Life, and that Life was the Light of humanity [Anthropos].*" [124]

*Ka Baibala* (The Bible) says, "*E nā punahele, e **aloha** kākou i kekahi i kekahi: no ka mea, no ke Akua mai ke **aloha**; 'o ka mea e **aloha** aku ana ua ho'ohānau 'ia mai ia e ke Akua, a ua 'ike nō 'o ia i ke Akua. 'O ka mea e **aloha** 'ole ana, 'a'ole ia i 'ike aku i ke Akua; no ka mea, he **Aloha ke Akua**.*"

"*Beloved, let us aloha one another, for aloha is of God; and everyone who displays aloha is born of God and knows God. He who does not aloha does not know God, for **God is Aloha**.*" 1 John 4:7-8.

'Īo is the God of Aloha and the God of the Bible. May we return to our True God again.

**Aloha Ke Akua**!

'Amene, 'Āmama Ua Noa!

# Bibliography

Allen, H. *The Betrayal of Lili'uokalani*. Glendale, CA: Mutual, 1982

Alpers, A. *The World of the Polynesians*. 1970; rpt. Auckland, N.Z.: Oxford University Press, 1987

Baker, H. *Behind the Tattooed Face*. New Zealand: Cape Catley Ltd., 1975

Beckwith, M. *Hawaiian Mythology*. 1940; rpt. Honolulu: University of Hawai'i Press, 1970

———. ed. *Kumulipo*. 1951; rpt. Honolulu: University Press of Hawai'i

Best, E. *The Maori As He Was*. Wellington, N.Z.: A.R. Shearer, Government Printer, 1934

———. *Maori Religion and Mythology*. No. 10-11. *Dominion Museum Bulletin*. Wellington, N.Z.: W.A.G. Skinner, Government Printer, 1924

———. The Maori School of Learning. Wellington, N.Z.: W.A.G. Skinner, Government Printer, 1923

———. *The Astronomical Knowledge of the Maori*. No. 3. *Dominion Museum Bulletin*. Wellington, N.Z.: W.A.G. Skinner, Government Printer, 1922

Bingham, H. *A Residence of Twenty-One Years in the Sandwich Islands*. Hartford: Hezekiah Huntington, 1847

Binney, J. *Redemption Songs*. Auckland University Press, 1995

Brandewie, E. *Wilhelm Schmidt and the Origin of the Idea of God*. Lanham, M.D.: University Press of America, 1983

Buck, P. *The Coming of the Maori*. Christchurch, N.Z.: Whitcombe & Tombs Ltd., 1949

———. *Vikings of the Pacific*. Chicago: University of Chicago Press, 1959

Cachola, J. *Kamehameha III: Kauikeaouli*. Honolulu: Kamehameha Schools Press, 1995

Cook, C. *The Providential Life & Heritage of Henry Obookiah*. Waimea, HI: Pa'a Studios, 2015

Cruikshank, G. *'Io Origins*. Whangarei: 1998

Curtis C. *Builders of Hawai'i*. Honolulu: Kamehameha Schools Press, 1966

Davis, C. *The Life And Times Of Patuone*. Auckland, N.Z.: Steam Printing Co., 1876

Daws, G. *Shoal of Time*. Honolulu: University of Hawai'i Press, 1968

De Bovis, E., Craig R. trans. *Tahitian Society Before the Arrival of the Europeans*. Hawaii: Brigham Young University Press, 1976

Dougherty, M. *To Steal A Kingdom*. Waimanalo, Hi. : Island Style Press, 1992

Dwight, E. *Memoirs of Henry Obookiah*. Ed. Wolfe, E. Honolulu: Woman's Board of Missions for the Pacific Islands, 1990

Emerson, O.P. *Pioneer Days in Hawai'i*. New York: Doubleday, Doran & Co., 1928

Feher, J. *Hawai'i: A Pictorial History*. Honolulu: Bishop Museum, 1969

Fornander, A. *An Account of the Polynesian Race*. 3 vols. London, 1878-1885; rpt. Rutland, Vt. : Charles E. Tuttle Co., 1969

———. *Fornander Collection of Hawaiian Antiquities and Folk-lore*. vol.IV of the *Memoirs of the Bernice Pauahi Bishop Museum*. ed. Thrum, T. Honolulu: Bishop Museum, 1916-1917

———. Fornander Collection of Hawaiian Antiquities and Folk-lore. vol. V of the *Memoirs of the Bernice Pauahi Bishop Museum*. ed. Thrum,T. Honolulu: Bishop Museum, 1918-1919

———. *Fornander Collection of Hawaiian Antiquities and Folk-lore*. vol. VI of the *Memoirs of the Bernice Pauahi Bishop Museum*. Honolulu: Bishop Museum, 1919-1920

Gessler, C. *Hawai'i, Isles of Enchantment*. N.Y.: D. Appleton-Century, 1937

Gough, B. ed., *To the Pacific and Arctic with Beechey: The Journal of Lieutenant George Peard of H.M.S. Blossom,*

*1825-1828*. London: The Hakluyt Society, 1973

Grant, K., Bendure, G., Friary, N., Gorry, C. *Hawaii*. Oakland, CA: Lonely Planet, 2005

Gutmanis, J., *Na Pule Kahiko: Ancient Hawaiian Prayers*. Honolulu: Editions Limited, 1983

Handy, E.S.C. *Polynesian Religion*. Bul. 34. *Bishop Museum*. Honolulu: Bishop Museum, 1927

–––. "Religion and Education." in *Ancient Hawaiian Civilization, A Series of Lectures*. Ed. Pratt, H. Honolulu: Kamehameha Schools, 1933

–––. *The Hawaiian Cult of 'Io*. vol. 50-51 *Journal of the Polynesian Society*. Wellington: The Polynesian Society, 1941

Handy, E.S.C. and Pukui, M.K. *The Polynesian Family System in Ka'ū, Hawai'i*. Wellington, N.Z.: Polynesian Society, 1958

Henry, T. *Ancient Tahiti*. Honolulu: Bishop Museum Press, 1928

Honolulu Star Bulletin. *All About Hawai'i*. Honolulu: Honolulu Star Bulletin, Feb. 1936

Hunnewell, J. *Bibliography of the Hawaiian Islands*, Intro. Boston: A. A. Kingman, 1869

'Ī'ī, J. *Fragments of Hawaiian History*. Trans. Pukui, M. Honolulu: Bishop Museum Press, 1959

International Bible Society. *The Holy Bible, New International Version*. Grand Rapids, MI: Zondervan, 1984

Irwin, G. *The Prehistoric Exploration and Colonisation of the Pacific*. Cambridge, U.K.: Cambridge University Press, 1992

Johnson, R. and Mahelona, J. *Nā Inoa Hōkū*. Honolulu: Topgallant Publishing, 1975

Kamakau, S. *Ka Moolelo O Na Kamehameha*. Honolulu: Ka Nupepa Kuokoa, March 28, 1868

Kamakau, S. *Ke Aupuni Mō'ī*. Honolulu: Kamehameha School Press, 2001

Kamakau, S. *Ruling Chiefs of Hawai'i*. Trans. Pukui, M., et al. Honolulu: Kamehameha School Press, 1961

Kamakau, S. *Tales and Traditions of the People of Old*. Trans. Pukui, M. Ed. Barre're, D. Honolulu: Bishop Museum Press, 1991

Kanahele, G. *Kū Kanaka*. Honolulu: University of Hawai'i Press, 1986

Kane, H. *The Voyagers*. Bellevue, WA.: WhaleSong, 1991

Kawaharada, D. *1992 Voyage: Sail to Ra'iatea*. Polynesian Voyaging Society, http://pvs.kcc.hawaii.edu/1992/raiatea.html

Kepelino. *Kepelino's Traditions of Hawai'i*. Bulletin 95. *Bernice P. Bishop Museum*. Ed. Beckwith, M. 1932; rpt. Millwood, N.Y.: Kraus Reprint Co., 1978

———. Kepelino's *"Hawaiian Collection": His "Hooiliili Havaii,"* Pepa I. vol. 11. *The Hawaiian Journal of History*. Trans. Kirtley, B. & Mookini, E. Ed. Jackson, F. 1858; rpt. Honolulu: Hawaiian Historical Society, 1977

Kikawa, D. *Perpetuated In Righteousness, 4th Ed.* Hawai'i: Aloha Ke Akua, 1994

Kikawa, D. *God of Light, God of Darkness*. Hawai'i: Aloha Ke Akua, 2008

Kirkwood, C. *Te Arikinui and The Millennium of Waikato*. N.Z.: Turongo House, 2001

Kuykendall, R.S. *The Hawaiian Kingdom*. vol. II. Honolulu: University of Hawai'i Press, 1953

Kuykendall, R.S. *The Hawaiian Kingdom*. vol. III. Honolulu: University of Hawai'i Press, 1967

Lili'uokalani, L. *Hawai'i's Story by Hawai'i's Queen*. Honolulu: Mutual Publishing, 1990

Lili'uokalani, L. *The Kumulipo*. Boston: Lee and Shepard, 1897

Loomis, A. *By Faith*. Honolulu: Offset Printing House, 1980

Loomis, A. *To All People*. Tennessee: Hawai'i Conference of the United Church of Christ, 1970

Malo, D. *Hawaiian Antiquities*. Trans. Emerson, N. Honolulu: Bishop Museum Press, 1951

Marocco, J. *Hawaii's Great Awakening*. Bartimaeus Publishing. Kahului, Hi. , 1991

Martin, L. *The Testimony of Yeshua*, Gabriel Bible Version, https://www.amazon.com/The-Testimony-of-Yeshua-ebook/dp/B004QS93CI/Kindle

Masse, Carter, and Somers. *Waha'ula Heiau*. University of Hawai'i Press, 1991

McAllister, J.G. *Archaeology of O'ahu*. Bulletin 104. *Bernice P. Bishop Museum*. 1933; rpt. Millwood, N.Y.: Kraus Reprint Co., 1971

Milner, G.B. *Samoan Dictionary*. 1966. rpt. Samoa: Gov't. of American Samoa, 1979

Mitchell, D. *Resource Units in Hawaiian Culture*. Honolulu: The Kamehameha Schools Press, 1982

Mitchell, R. *From God to God*. 3 Books. O'ahu: 1979

Montgomery, H. *Christus Redemptor*. MacMillan, 1906

Moon, P. *Tohunga:Hohepa Kereopa*. David Ling Pub., 2003

Mulholland. *Hawai'i's Religions*. Rutland, Vt.: C.E. Tuttle Co., 1970

The Native Hawaiian Land Trust Task Force. *The Prophetic Vision of Ke'ōpūolani, The Sacred Queen of Hawai'i*. Hawai'i: Hawaiian Almanac Publishing, 1982

Nāwahī , J. *Ke Aloha Aina*. Ka Leo O Ka Lahui, vol. II, Num. 682. Honolulu: April 12, 1893

Nicholas, J.L. Narrative of a Voyage to New Zealand, 2 vols. London: James Black and Son, 1817

Norman, P., To'o M. *Knowledge of the God of Creation*. Manuscript

Noyes, M. *Polynesian Star Catalog: Revised*. Honolulu: Barefeet Prod., 2011

Oliver, D. *Ancient Tahitian Society 3 vols*. Honolulu: University Press of Hawaii, 1974

Orbell, M. *The Natural World of the Maori*. Dobbs Ferry, N.Y.: Sheridan House, 1985

Pei Te Hurinui. *King Potatau*. Wellington N.Z.: The Polynesian Society, 1959

Pettazzoni, R. *The All Knowing God; Researches into Early Religion and Culture*. London: Methuen, 1956

Piercy, L. *Hawaii Truth Stranger Than Fiction*. Honolulu: Fisher, 1985

–––. *Hawai'i's Missionary Saga*. Honolulu: Mutual Publishing, 1992

Potter, N. & Kasdon, L. *Hawai'i Our Island State*. Ohio: Charles E. Merrill Books, 1964

Pratt, G. *Samoan Dictionary*. Samoa: London Missionary Society Press, 1862

Pukui, M. & Elbert, S. *Hawaiian-English Dictionary*. Honolulu: University of Hawai'i Press, 1957

Pukui, M., Haertig, E.W., Lee, C. *Nānā I Ke Kumu*. 2 vols. Honolulu: Hui Hanai, 1972

Richards, W. *Memoir of Ke'ōpūolani*. Boston: Crocker & Brewster, 1825

Rose, R. *Hawai'i: The Royal Isles*. Honolulu: Bishop Museum, 1980

Ryan, P.M. *The New Dictionary of Modern Maori*. Auckland, N.Z.: Heinemann, 1974

Schmitt, R. *Historical Statistics of Hawai'i*. Honolulu: University of Hawai'i Press, 1977

-———. *The Missionary Censuses of Hawai'i*. Honolulu: Bishop Museum, 1973

Schmidt, W. *The Origin and Growth of Religion*. Trans. Rose, H. J. London: Methuen & Co., 1935

Shortland, E. *Traditions and Superstitions of the New Zealanders*. 1856; rpt. New York: AMS Press, 1980

Siers, J. *Tonga*. Wellington, N.Z.: Millwood Press, 1978

Sinclair, K. ed. *The Oxford Illustrated History of New Zealand*. Auckland, N.Z.: Oxford University Press

Silverman, J. *Ka'ahumanu, Molder of Change*. Honolulu: Friends of the Judiciary History Cntr. of Hawai'i, 1987

Smith, P. *Hawaiki: The Original Home of the Maori*. N.Z.: Whitcombe and Tombs, 1904

Smith, P. *Journal of the Polynesian Society*. supplement. vol. 29-30. Wellington, N.Z.: The Polynesian Society, 1920

Sorrenson, M.P.K. *Maori Origins and Migrations*. Auckland University Press, 1979

Sterling, E. & Summers, C. Editors. *Sites of O'ahu*. Honolulu: Bishop Museum, 1978

Stimson, J.F. *The Cult of Kiho-tuma*. Bulletin 111. *Bernice P. Bishop Museum*. Honolulu: The Museum, 1933

Taylor, C. "Tales About Hawai'i." *Honolulu Star Bulletin*. Newspaper. Honolulu: Monday, June 19, 1961

Taylor, E.A. "The Cult of 'Iolani." *Paradise of the Pacific*. Dec. 1931

Taylor, P. *Kapi'olani: A Memorial*. Honolulu: Grieve, 1897

Te Haupapa-o-tane. *"Io, The Supreme God, and Other Gods Of The Maori*. vol. 29-30. *Journal of the Polynesian Society*. Wellington, N.Z.: The Polynesian Society, 1920

Tregear, E. *Maori-Polynesian Comparative Dictionary*. Wellington, N.Z.: Lyon & Blair, 1891

Thrum, T. *Hawaiian Folk Tales*. Chicago: A.C. McClurg & Co., 1912

Valeri, V. trans. Wissing, P. *Kingship and Sacrifice, Ritual and Society in Ancient Hawaii*. Chicago: University of Chicago Press, 1985

Viola, F. *Pagan Christianity*. Tyndale House, 2007

Whatahoro, H.T. *The Lore of the Whare-Wananga*. pt. 1. vol. 3-4. *Memoirs of the Polynesian Society*. Trans. Smith, P. New Plymoth, N.Z.: Thomas Avery, 1913

White, J. *The Ancient History of the Maori, His Mythology and Traditions*. vols. 1 & 2. Wellington: George Didsbury, Government Printer, 1887

Williams, R. *To Raise a Voice in Praise: The Revivalist Mission of John Henry Wise, 1889-1896*. The Hawaiian Journal of History

Wise, J. and Case, H. *True God of the Hawaiians Returns in 'Square Box,' According to Old Prophecy*, Honolulu Start Bulletin, Sat. Nov. 10, 1923, section 2.

Wisniewski, R. *The Rise and Fall of the Hawaiian Kingdom*. Honolulu: Pacific Basin Ent., 1979

# Endnotes

1.  Norman & To'o, *Knowledge of the God of Creation*, p. 25
2.  Beckwith, *The Kumulipo*, p. 12
3.  Allen, *The Betrayal of Lili'uokalani*, pp. 117-118
4.  Fornander, *Acct. Poly. Race,* vol. 1, p. 60
5.  Fornander, *Acct. Poly. Race, vol. 1*, p. 60
6.  Beckwith, *Hawaiian Mythology*, p. 370
7.  Handy, *Polynesian Religion*, Bulletin 34, p. 96
8   Handy, Journal of the Polynesian Society: The Hawaiian Cult of 'Io, p.135
9   ibid.
10. Buck, *The Coming of the Maori*, pp. 443-444
11. Handy, Polynesian Religion, Bernice P. Bishop Museum, Bulletin 34, p. 95
12. Watahoro, Smith Trans. The Lore of the Whare-wananga, p. vi
13. Best, *Maori Religion and Mythology*, p. 94
    Whatahoro, *The Lore of the Whare-Wananga*, p. 106
14. Best, *Maori Religion and Mythology*, p. 90
15. Handy, *Ancient Haw'n Civilization*, pp. 117-118
    Best, *Maori Religion and Mythology*, p. 94
    Taylor, *Paradise of the Pacific*, Dec. 1931, p. 78
    For., *Acct. Poly. Race, vol. 1*, p. 61
16. Handy, *The Hawaiian Cult of 'Io*, pp. 142-3, 148
17. Allen, *The Betrayal of Lili'uokalani*, pg. 387, 391
18. ibid.
19. ibid. p. 146
20. Watahoro, Smith Trans. *The Lore of the Whare-wananga*, p. vi
21. Malo, *Hawaiian Antiquities*, p. 276

22. Johnson and Mahelona, *Nā Inoa Hōkū*, p.13
23. Noyes, M., *Polynesian Star Catalog: Revised*
24. https://www.mauiculture.net/mookuauhau/index.html
25 *'Iolani* Newspaper, May 1993
26. MidWeek Magazine, West Oahu News, 11/17/2010
27. Roy, *Viewpoint: Ahuʻena Heiau*, Ke Ola mag., Hawaiʻi Ed., July-Aug. 2014, pp. 62, 64
28. Ngata, *The 'Io Cult*, pp. 336-337
29. Shirres, Te Tangata, p.113
30. ibid. p.110
31. ibid. p. 111
32. ibid. p. 108
33. Davis, *Life and Times of Patuone*, 1876, pp. 132-133
34. Best, *Maori Religion and Mythology Part 1*, pp. 146-147
35. ibid.
36. Robinson, *Tohunga*, p. 94
37. ibid, p. 277
38. ibid, pp. 278-27
39. Cruickshank, 'Io Origins, p. 36
40. Best, *Maori Religion and Mythology*, pp. 91-92
41. Best, Maori Religion and Mythology Part 1
42. Stimson, *Tuamotuan Religion*, p. 74-79
43. Taylor, *Paradise of the Pacific*, Dec. 1931, p. 78
44. ibid. p. 147
45. James, *Myth and Ritual in the Ancient Near East*, p.127
46. Stimson, *Tuamotuan Religion*, p.77
47. For., Acct. Poly. Race, vol. 1, footnote, p. 179
48. Moon, *Tohunga: Hohepa Kereopa*, Kindle location 838
49. ibid., Kindle location 1278
50. Robinson, *Tohunga*, p. 278
51. Norman & Toʻo, *Knowledge of the God of Creation*, p.26
52. Norman & Toʻo, *Knowledge of the God of Creation*, p. 25
53. Best, The Maori School of Learning, pp. 4-5
54. For., *Acct. Poly. Race, vol. 1*, p. 209

55. Both Ahu'enaTaylor and Malia Craver are descended from the line of Pā'ao

56. Buck, *Vikings*, pp. 262-263

57. Masse, Waha'ula Heiau, p. 21

58. Fornander, *Acct. Poly. Race, vol. 1*, p.129

59. ibid., *vol. 2*, p. 63

60. Montgomery, *Christus*, p. 97
Malo, *Antiquities*, pp. 56-57

61. Kamakau, *Ruling Chiefs of Hi.*, pp. 232, 236

62. Kamakau, *Ruling Chiefs*, p. 232
Sterling/*Summers, Sites of O*'ahu, p. 291

63. Sterling/Summers, *Sites*, p. 292

64. McAllister, *Archaeology of O'ahu*, p. 81

65. ibid., p. 71

66. Malo, *Antiquities*, pp. 172-173, 186
Masse, Waha'ula Heiau, p. 43

67. Montgomery, *Christus*, pp. 95, 97
Kamakau, *Ruling Chiefs*, pp. 229-232
Malo, *Antiquities*, p. 62, 64

68. Emerson, *Pioneer Days in Hi.*, p. 4

69. Piercy, *Hawai'i Truth Stranger Than Fiction*, p. 40

70. Pukui, Nānā, p. 122/Fornander, Acct. Poly. Race, vol. 1, p. 163

71. Wise, *True God of the Hawaiians Returns in 'Square Box,' According to Old Prophecy*, Honolulu Start Bulletin, Sat. Nov. 10, 1923, section 2.

72. Gessler, *Hawai'i, Isles of Enchantment*, p. 58.

73. Lili'uokalani, *The Kumulipo*, Intro.

74. Fornander, Collection of Hawaiian Folk-lore, p. 158

75. Honolulu Star Bulletin, *All About Hawai'i*, Feb. 1936 pp. 28-29.

76. Mitchell, *From God to God*, p. 33 / the Hawaiian Music Foundation Web site. http://www.hawaiimusicmuseum.org/honorees/2000/chanters.html

77 Gough, ed., *To the Pacific and Arctic with Beechey: The Journal of Lieutenant Gorge Peard of H.M.S. Blossom, 1825-1828*, p. 135.

78. Kalākaua, D. *The Legends and Myths of Hawaii*, p. 270 Kindle Edition
79. ibid., p. 271
80. ibid., p. 274
81. ibid., pp. 273-274).
82. Brewster, *Memoir of Keopuolani*, p. 17.
83. Piercy, Hawaiʻi's Missionary Saga, p. 19
84. Hunnewell, Brigham, Dole, *Bibliography of the Hawaiian Islands*, Introduction
85. Taylor, *Kapiʻolani: A Memorial*, pp. 15-16.
86. Loomis; Kawaiahaʻo
87. Dwight, *Memoirs of Henry Obookiah*
88. Loomis, By Faith, pp. 4-5
89. Extracts from a journal supposed to have been written By Elisha Loomis; Gulick
90. Gessler, *Hawaiʻi, Isles of Enchantment*, p. 58.
91. Binney, *Redemption Songs*, pg. 352
92. Handy, *Ancient Hawʻn Civilization*, pp. 117-118
    Best, *Maori Religion and Mythology*, p. 94
    Taylor, *Paradise of the Pacific*, Dec. 1931, p. 78
    Fornander, *Acct. Poly. Race, vol. 1*, p. 61
93. Handy, Journal of the Polynesian Society: The Hawaiian Cult of ʻĪo, p. 158
94. Johnson and Mahelona, *Nā Inoa Hōkū*, p.13
95. Noyes, M., *Polynesian Star Catalog: Revised*
96. Buck, *Vikings*, p. 274
97. Elsmore, *Like Them That Dream*, p. 25
98. ibid. p.108
99. Turongo House, *Tawhiao – King or Prophet, pp. 188-192*
100. Handy, *Ancient Hawaiian Civilization*, pp. 43-45
101. ibid
102. ibid., p. 444
103. Turongo House, *Tawhiao – King or Prophet*
     Turongo House, *Koroki My King*
104. Kamakau, *Ruling Chiefs of Hawaiʻi*, pp. 263-264
     Kamakau, *Ke Aupuni Mōʻī*, pp. 12-13

105. Piercy, *Hawaii Truth*, p. 21

106. The Constitution of 1840

107. The Native Hawaiian Land Trust Task Force, *The Prophetic Vision of Keʻopuolani, The Sacred Queen of Hawaii*

108. ibid.

109. Mitchell, *From God to God*, pp. 48-53

110. Allen, *Betrayal*, p. 392

111. ibid. p.184

112. ibid., pp. 299,300

113. ibid. p. 190

114. ibid. p.190

115. ibid. p.343

116. Norman & Toʻo, *Knowledge of the God of Creation*, p.26

117. Notes of Pei Te Hurinui Jones, Allexander Turnbull Library

118. ibid. p.107

119. ibid., p.207

120. Dougherty, *To Steal*, pp. 81,103
     Piercy, *Hawaii Truth*, p.14

121. Daws, *Shoal of Time*, p. 251

122. Allen, *The Betrayal of Liliʻuokalani*, p. 268

123. Daws, *Shoal of Time*, pp. 246-249

124. Martin, *The Testimony of Yeshua*, Gabriel Bible Version, https://www.amazon.com/The-Testimony-of-Yeshua-ebook/dp/B004QS93CI/Kindle

Made in the USA
Monee, IL
19 April 2025

e155d11b-a6db-4447-b067-73fe874aa797R01